▪ The Post-Classical Predicament

Music advisor to Northeastern University Press
Gunther Schuller

The Post-Classical
Predicament

· *Essays on Music and Society* ·

Joseph Horowitz

Northeastern University Press
Boston

Library of Congress Cataloging-in-Publication Data

Horowitz, Joseph, 1948–
    The post-classical predicament : essays on music and society /
Joseph Horowitz.
        p.   cm.
    Includes bibliographical references and index.
    ISBN 1-55553-218-7 (acid-free paper)
    1. Music and society.   2. Music—United States—20th century—
History and criticism.   I. Title.
ML3795.H78   1995
781.6'8'0973—dc20   94-41835

Designed by Amy Bernstein

Composed in Adobe Garamond 3 by Graphic Composition, Inc., Athens, Georgia. Printed and bound by Thomson-Shore, Inc., Dexter, Michigan. The paper is Glatfelter Supple Opaque Recycled, an acid-free sheet.

MANUFACTURED IN THE UNITED STATES OF AMERICA
99   98   97   96   95   5   4   3   2   1

· *Preface and Acknowledgments*

During four tortured years as a young *New York Times* music critic, I would pore over my reviews every summer, worrying about what I had said and what damage I had done, searching for signs of intellectual fortitude and improved writing skills. In later years, I worried less and reread nothing. Preparing the present essay collection, I reencountered fifteen years of magazine work with a pleasurable curiosity. With a few exceptions, I found the earlier pieces impossible, but this came as no surprise. Certain complaints about the fate of classical music as a late twentieth-century anachronism were, I learned, a steadier leitmotif than I had recalled. At the same time, I discovered a trajectory: a mounting aversion to hermetic music talk. Music and society—the history of our concert institutions and of their interaction with artists, with audiences, and with the urban scene—became my topic. This same trajectory ultimately propelled me toward my current job as executive director of the Brooklyn Philharmonic, resident orchestra of the remarkable and idiosyncratic Brooklyn Academy of Music.

My four books previous to this one chart a somewhat similar course. *Conversations with Arrau* (1980) mainly sticks to music and the piano; at the same time, it contrasts the artistic efflorescence of Weimar Germany, in which the young Arrau was a fortunate participant, with later cultural communities more blurred and dispersed. *Understanding Toscanini* (1987) is a revisionist social history of American concert life, a jeremiad lamenting twentieth-century decline and fall (and chronicling the music appreciation movement and other interwar developments to which I frequently refer in the essays at hand). *The Ivory Trade* (1990), a coda to *Understanding Toscanini,* is an up-to-date hinterlands report. In *Wagner Nights* (1994), looking backward a full century, I find solace in fin de siècle ferment—but also inspiration.

The older essays in this collection are more extensively reedited than the newer ones. They remain different, of course, from what I would write today. (The indignation of *Understanding Toscanini* is inflamed by an experience of betrayal: as a young adult, I discovered that the world of music that I had come to love as a child was confined and diminished by circumstances beyond my control. I no longer feel as angry.)

The helpful original editors of the essays that follow included Sedgwick Clark at *Keynote* Magazine, Jim Oestreich at *Opus* and the *New York Times* Arts & Leisure section, and Barbara Epstein at the *New York Review of Books.* I am also indebted to Bill Frohlich and Ann Twombly of Northeastern University Press, and to my agent, Elizabeth Kaplan. As I write these words they are taking me away from Agnes and Bernie, my understanding wife and son.

· Contents

The Post-Classical Predicament

· *Introduction*

The Post-Classical Predicament

The young folk nowadays are not epicures. Wine palates they have not; cocktails and the common consumption of spirits have banished all sense of taste values. They are in too much of a hurry to dance or to ride, to sit long at table and dine with discrimination.

The number of cheap, quick-fire food hells is appalling. One understands during the mid-day rush that a glass of milk and a slice of pie suffice, but when the day's toil is over and the upper town achieved, then we expect leisure and elegance, taste in the evening menu. They are seldom to be found. Noisy bands of music-makers, ill-cooked food and hastily gobbled, shrieking instead of conversation, and then—dancing. This is the order of the evening. . . .

Eating and drinking are rapidly entering the category of the lost fine arts. Bolting, guzzling, gum chewing, and film pictures have driven them away.

Some day, say hopeful prophets, they will return. I doubt it. Our age is too materialistic.

The author of these lines was James Gibbons Huneker. The year was 1915, when Huneker was fifty-eight years old. The most flamboyant American critic of his time, he had also proved the most prescient. For decades he had been the very herald of modernism. His enthusiasms included Hauptmann, Joyce, Mallarmé, Munch, Strindberg, and Wedekind. He was no sentimentalist. He looked forward. His memories of fin de siècle New York cannot be written off as nostalgia.

Huneker arrived in New York in 1886. He lived at Madison

Avenue and Seventy-sixth Street in a tenth-floor apartment from which he could see the East River, the Hudson, and the Statue of Liberty. His favorite haunts included the Lower East Side, a place festering with anarchists and bohemians. In Justus Schwab's saloon, on Tompkins Square, he met Ambrose Bierce and Emma Goldman, debated the merits of Dostoyevsky and Nietzsche, and played the "Marsellaise" and the "Internationale" on a smoke-stained piano with rattling keys. At Maisel's Bookstore, on East Grand, he devoured great literature, old and new. "The East Side is an omnivorous reader. Stupendous is the amount of books studied and digested; books of solid worth, not 'best sellers' or other flimflam," he testified in 1915—by which time, however, he found reading habits much degraded.

The reckless scope of Huneker's criticism embraced everything from poetry to painting. Essentially, however, he was a musician, and his essential topic was music. Slightly to the west of his East Side haunts, he equally frequented the Union Square neighborhood: the very hub of musical New York, of music in America. Here he found not only musicians, including a number of great ones, but also thriving German theaters, beer saloons with sawdust on the floor, and restaurants whose leisurely dining regime he would longingly recall twenty years later: Maurer's, Moulds', Brubacher's, Fleischmann's, and—"best of all, a certain place presided over by a blue-eyed, rosy-cheeked young German, whose amiability was proverbial, whose beer was perfection"—August Lüchow's.

The habitués of these establishments included the prodigious Wagnerian tenor Albert Niemann, the supreme singing actor of his generation, "a drinker that would have pleased Pantagruel." Niemann would down cocktails from a beer glass all night until noon the next day. He was also fond of a concoction combining brandy, ginger ale, and absinthe. This was the invention of his drinking partner Otto Floersheim, of the *Musical Courier.* Niemann's operatic partner was the regal Lilli Lehmann, who knew everything and everybody, and who frequented Lienau's. Antonin

Dvořák, who lived down the block on East Seventeenth, was in Huneker's opinion one of the great imbibers of all time, a man "as dangerous to a moderate drinker as a false beacon is to a ship-wrecked sailor"; he chased cocktails and beer with Slivavitch. Another composer on the scene was Victor Herbert, a model of bon-homie. The pianists included Rafael Joseffy, who had studied with Liszt, and whom Huneker (who had studied with Joseffy) called "that fixed star in the pianistic firmament, one who refuses to descend to earth and please the groundlings"; and Moriz Rosenthal, who had studied with Liszt and Joseffy and was in Huneker's opinion "the Napoleon, the conqueror among virtuosi." Huneker did not document the conviviality of these Union Square regulars, or of the legendary violinist Eugène Ysaÿe, who liked Moulds'. But he considered another Moulds' patron, the poet Frank Saltus, the greatest living master of "human discourse" after Oscar Wilde. The place was crammed, as well, with famous actors. William Steinway, who liked Lienau's, was both a piano manufacturer and a leading political power broker. Of the attendant critics, Albert Steinberg of the *Tribune,* also an inveterate gambler, possessed "a wit that was positively malignant"; he "would place his surgical steel on your sorest place, and your vanity bled." Huneker himself, needless to say, was a world-class raconteur; a reporter once likened him to "the Encyclopedia Britannica suddenly becoming vocal and giving tongue with all its potential eloquence."

This was one form of New York's turn-of-the-century cultural life. Another, in the same neighborhood, and attracting the same participants, inhabited Steinway Hall, the Academy of Music, and the National Conservatory of Music. Some twenty and forty blocks uptown, respectively, were the Metropolitan Opera and Carnegie Hall. A single musician dominated all this activity, uptown and down: the conductor Anton Seidl, of whom Huneker wrote, "The man with his elemental energy seemed a sort of demigod. . . . He had the sort of personality that overpowered through sheer existing. Without any apparent volition on his part, he made one feel that he was a distinguished man—a man among men."

Seidl galvanized the fifty-year-old New York Philharmonic. At the Met, where he conducted from 1885 until his death in 1897, he created a shrine for Wagner—with Bayreuth, the leading Wagner house in the world. He was taciturn, romantically remote and unworldly. And yet, in New York in the 1890s, musicians of genius remained public figures. Every afternoon Seidl rode the Fourth Avenue streetcar—the drivers and brakeman knew him as "the Professor"—to Fleischmann's, at Tenth and Broadway, there to read the newspapers and puff cigars. At Coney Island's Brighton Beach, where he conducted daily in the summer, he promenaded every afternoon at five. Reviewing a charity concert Seidl conducted for an audience of eight thousand, the *Morning Journal* called him "pre-eminently a man of the people." "No conductor was ever so popular with a mass of people in this city," remarked the *Sun* in 1898. "He was well-known by sight to more New Yorkers than any other musician in this city, and he was recognized everywhere in public."

Seidl spoke English, took American citizenship, and praised democracy. In his speeches, he espoused playing "good music for good men and women," by which he meant free or inexpensive Beethoven, Liszt, and Wagner for those who had never heard an orchestra. "That man, who asks for not playing some classical works at the popular concerts," he orated, "is not a democrat, is not a republican, not an—American." Like his friend Dvořák, with whom he would sit in sphinxlike silence at Fleischmann's upstairs round table, Seidl understood classical music as a kind of sublimated folk art. That is why Dvořák, during his historic three-year directorship of the National Conservatory, studied African-American and American Indian music; he tried to point the way for American composers in search of a recognizable New World idiom. Seidl himself was composing an Indianist opera, based on the Hiawatha legend, when he died. The absorption of folk sources, he assumed, would generate a concert language that all Americans could know and understand.

In New York, Seidl's circle included Robert Ingersoll, the "Great Agnostic," who influentially championed women's suffrage and birth control; Richard Watson Gilder, among the leading magazine editors of the day; and Carl Schurz, the reform leader and statesman. A young actor and playwright named Francis Neilson, a surrogate son to Seidl, later wrote:

> Almost any day of the week, between the hours of eleven and one, a sprinkling of men connected with the drama, literature, journalism, and art might be found in the barrooms of Broadway's big hotels. . . . In those days the man of business, the scientist, the doctor and lawyer would be found in the company of artists, glad to be in close touch with them and to dispense their quips and sallies to an ever widening circle. . . . What raconteurs they were!

Huneker confirmed that such places as Moulds' were centers "for actors, writers, artists, musicians, as well as business and professional men."

The composer and critic Arthur Farwell—like Victor Herbert, a Seidl protégé—had occasion to look back at the 1890s half a century later. In a 1944 article in the *Musical Quarterly,* he lamented "the advent of the more dazzling but, as many hold, less sympathetic virtuoso conductor"—as opposed to Anton Seidl, whose "known love for New York" inspired "downright affection, rather than admiration or awe." Seidl's spell, Farwell continued, "tinged the atmosphere and the consciousness of the city with a peculiarly individual and glowing quality of feeling such as it has not known before or since." Musical New York of the late nineteenth century, as recalled by Farwell, or by Huneker or Neilson, was in fact much different from what it became mere decades later. The Metropolitan Opera never served as lofty a purpose as during the "German seasons" of 1884 to 1891, or assembled such an array of talent as during the "Golden Age" beginning in 1891–92. Never would recent or contemporary symphonies and operas loom so large in the city's musical consciousness (and conscience), or would issues in American music so dominate sophisticated public discussion and debate. Never again would classical music prove so organic to intellectual life in general, or to the culture at large.

Ten years later, this organic integration of music and society was already fracturing. Gustav Mahler, who arrived in New York in 1907, and Arturo Toscanini, who came in 1908, were febrile embodiments of the "virtuoso conductor" Farwell decried. Lured to America by vast sums of cash, neither came to stay. Both remained strangers to Union Square. Mahler, had he lived longer, might have made an enduring contribution: his second New York Philharmonic season, 1910–11, included five American works (his first, comprising forty-six concerts, had included none). At the time of his death in 1911, however, Mahler was still an interloper, based in Vienna.

Toscanini, based in Italy, attracted a new kind of attention, signaling a new ambience for art. The anecdotes he generated did not, like those told of Seidl, originate on New York's sidewalks or in its restaurants and cafés. They fostered a study in the foibles and eccentricities of individual genius: fabled memory, fits of temper, quaint superstitiousness. Never had Seidl inspired such news items as these:

> It is well understood here . . . that Mr. Slezak's failure to appear was the culmination of certain difficulties in existence for some time between Mr. Slezak and Mr. Toscanini, and that, preceding last evening's performance Mr. Toscanini stated, simply but emphatically, that he would not conduct if Mr. Slezak sang.

> Gossip has it that the real reason for the *Tristan und Isolde* postponement last week was Arturo Toscanini's

anger at two of the principals who failed to appear at the rehearsal he had called.

Reports were circulated on Monday along Broadway and Fifth Avenue to the effect that the orchestra at the Metropolitan had struck and would not play any more under Toscanini, owing to his having insulted two members of their body.

Henry Krehbiel, the most comprehensive and profound chronicler of New York's turn-of-the-century musical life (and a frequent presence in the pages that follow), noticed the new ambience. Of opera in New York between 1908 and 1918, he observed:

During the period of which I am writing, even in journals of dignity and scholarly repute the gossip of the foyer and the dressing rooms of the chorus and ballet stood in higher esteem with the news editors than the comments of conscientious critics. . . . If in this [the newspapers] reflect the taste of their readers, it is a taste which they have instilled and cultivated, for it did not exist before the days of photo-engraving, illustrated supplements and press agents.

With Huneker and W. J. Henderson, Krehbiel presided over the most distinguished constellation of music critics ever to assemble in New York. By 1926 only Henderson was left to document Toscanini's New York Philharmonic debut. He wrote:

The concert of the Philharmonic Society last night in Carnegie Hall was one of those musical events which might well be turned over to the star descriptive reporter. It was not a concert at all; it was the return of the hero, a Roman triumph staged in New York and in modern dress. . . .

For these are days when the plain workaday utterance of music will not suffice for a populace incessantly de-

manding new ways of saying old truths and ready to sink
into apathy unless mental stimulants are liberally administered.

Reviews of Seidl had routinely concentrated on the music he
conducted, which was mainly recent or new. Toscanini, by comparison, was the main focus of attention, generating rites of worship no previous conductor had enjoyed. This new reverence for
performance supplanted interest in the creative act. Mahler and
Toscanini notwithstanding, audiences at the Met grew bored with
Wagner, whose operas—the works themselves, not the singers or
conductors—had hushed capacity houses in Seidl's day. The tenor
Carl Burrian, a distinguished Siegmund, Siegfried, and Tristan for
Mahler and Toscanini at the Met, testified in 1908:

> The Wagner performances are the least patronized by the
> public. The whole business apparently bores the audiences
> to death. . . . There is a constant coming and going; the
> spectators greet one another, look around them and see
> who is there. . . . After the long intermission one need
> only to glance in the boxes to see that by a few minutes
> after 11 there is a packing up of opera glasses in reticules
> and the start for home.

By the interwar decades, a new audience for classical music
had in fact congealed. The radio, the automobile, and the telephone had penetrated small-town America and spread the nation's
wealth. The five-day work week meant more leisure time for the
new middle classes; time for baseball and the movies—and for
museums and concerts. An eager consumerism spurred the acquisition of vacuum cleaners and refrigerators—and of higher
learning and knowledge of the arts. In music, the popularizing
impulse translated into radio concerts, record sales, and proliferating orchestras; according to one survey, the number of Ameri-

can orchestras increased from 17 before World War I to 270 by 1939.

To the socialist Charles Edward Russell, the symphony orchestra in 1927 seemed America's "foremost cultural asset," its "sign of honor among nations," its one "division of representative art" in which "achievement has gone beyond debate." These claims were both apt and misleading. Many newcomers to Bach and Beethoven were converted heart and soul. For the majority of the new audience, the attainment of new knowledge was shallower. From the standpoint of individual lives, this was, inherently, neither good nor bad. But the consequences for the cultural community were profound. What Virgil Thomson called the "music appreciation racket" inculcated that art was for museums, that great symphonies, paintings, and novels were the finished products of dead geniuses. Fixating on Great Performers, and the masterpieces they served, the music appreciators tutored the new audience to disdain American music and contemporary culture. In a period when jazz became America's most individual, most influential musical export, music appreciation shunned popular music as a menace. New York's great symphonic event of the 1890s—heralded and analyzed for weeks on end—had been the premiere of Dvořák's *New World* Symphony, with Seidl conducting and Dvořák the guest of honor. The great operatic event of the 1880s, with Seidl, Lilli Lehmann, and Albert Niemann, had been the United States premiere of *Tristan und Isolde,* before a tensely expectant packed house at the Met. In the 1930s, no classical music event seemed more important than another Toscanini performance of Beethoven's Fifth.

The new audience exasperated a new generation of American composers—and the antipathy was mutual. The modernism of the new composers was anti-Romantic, antireligious. The new audience sacralized great music. Seidl, it is true, had sacralized Wagner: Wagner's music demanded it. For devotees of *Parsifal,* sacralization was an aesthetic necessity. It suffused the Music of the Future, of which Wagner was part. Twentieth-century sacralization, by comparison, was a popular movement worshiping the music of the past. It validated no living composer as it validated Toscanini. "Prophet," "priest of enlightenment," "vehicle of revelation," he was the first conductor to become the world's most famous musician.

To the schism between musical life and intellectual life, between audience and composer, was added a schism between highbrow and low. Like sacralization, this was a nineteenth-century development transformed by twentieth-century popularization. Never before—before the microphone and Crosby, before Gershwin and Porter, before Ellington and swing—had there been anything like the popular music of the 1920s and 1930s, or the accompanying retrenchment of the classical establishment. Dvořák, in the 1890s, had mediated between high and low. He relished symphonies and plantation songs, operas and Stephen Foster. He assumed an organicity of music—all music—and society.

The Second World War was, like the First, a watershed for musical affairs. In the Old World, it shattered links to the past: to schools of composition and interpretation, to previous audiences. In the United States since World War II, "classical music" has been largely reconceived as a species of pretentious popular entertainment masquerading as fine art. What passed for classical music in other times is defined away. Today the term itself is either a misnomer or an anachronism. Gone and forgotten are the Seidls, Dvořáks, and Hunekers of Union Square days. At Lincoln Center, James Levine is not even a public presence. Seidl, his colleagues, and friends worried aloud about the fate of music in the contemporary United States. Does Levine?

Grievances of this sort permeate the essays that follow. Other essays look back at better times. Looking forward, I write appreciatively of the postmodern impulse in the opera stagings of Patrice Chéreau, and in Ken Russell's campy films about composers' lives. The liberating eclecticism of a Chéreau or Russell, of a Gidon Kremer or John Adams, the irreverence with which they revisit traditional texts and tropes, suggest strategies of post-classical reform. They hold out the promise of an aesthetically renewed post-classical music. They could actually make it possible for classical music, as in "The Music of Forest Lawn," to rest in peace.

1 · *Mozart as Midcult*

Mass Snob Appeal

Mozart, who died poor, was ever a fallible self-promoter. His actual life, his actual music, while not unappealing, mainly interested a cultivated elite. It took Peter Shaffer, two centuries later, to make Mozart irresistible to millions of classical music novices.

Shaffer's efficacious popularization strategy is two-faceted. First, he simplifies the subject matter. Compared to Mozart's original life, with all its messy detail, Shaffer's version, in his play *Amadeus,* is taut, schematic, marvelously theatrical. Compared to Mozart's symphonies and concertos, with their abstract content, Shaffer's samplings of the B-flat Wind Serenade, the D minor Piano Concerto, and the Sinfonia Concertante for Violin and Viola— all of which figure in the *Amadeus* film, directed by Milos Forman—are decked out in visual imagery so attractive and informative that we know exactly what to think and feel. A peerless confectioner, Shaffer makes even the pain of Mozart's penury or the stridence of his *Dies Irae* go down as easily as cough medicine in sweet syrup.

The second facet of Shaffer's popularization technique is the wrapping on the candy: it is itself a magnificent production, elaborate yet unmistakably tasteful. That is to say, unlike Hollywood's great-composer popularizations, *Amadeus* conspicuously aspires to the pretensions of high art. Utterly rejecting the careless vulgarity of *A Song to Remember* (with Cornel Wilde as Chopin) or *Song of Love* (with Paul Henreid as Schumann and Robert Walker as Brahms), Shaffer and Forman insist on sophisticated acting and production values; they are not opportunistic but sincere. Their pleasure in celebrating the "timeless" and "great" is palpable, even explicit. The higher the pedestal, the more they enjoy gazing aloft.

This potent hybridization of mass appeal and snob appeal is what Dwight Macdonald, in a landmark 1960 essay, called "midcult." Midcult possesses the essential qualities of mass culture—the formula, the built-in reaction—but "decently covers them with a cultural figleaf." It "pretends to respect the standards of high culture while in fact it waters them down and vulgarizes them." Not cynically, but sincerely, it "aspires to universality above all." Its "tepid ooze" is "spreading everywhere." Macdonald's examples include *The Old Man and the Sea, Our Town,* and Rodgers and Hammerstein.

As Macdonald implies and as *Amadeus* attests, a mere biography, no matter how august its subject, cannot qualify as midcult. Shaffer's Mozart treatment is more impressive, more "serious." He gives us not Mozart's life story, but (as he himself once put it) a "fantasia on events in Mozart's life." Like Pushkin, in his play *Mozart and Salieri,* and Rimsky-Korsakov, in his opera after the Pushkin, Shaffer takes as his starting point the legend that Mozart was poisoned by Vienna's court kapellmeister. But, unlike Pushkin or Rimsky-Korsakov, Shaffer extracts a universal question: "What is the relationship of creativity to personality?" Attentive to the sometimes scatological language of Mozart's letters and musical ditties, to his unworldly impracticality and uncanny compositional facility, he infers a portrait of the composer as a foolish man-child, almost an idiot savant. Shaffer's Salieri states the paradox in an indignant address to God: "You choose for your instrument a smutty boy." This catalyzes the *Amadeus* plot: the eminent, industrious Salieri, hungry for an immortality he knows will never be his, envies the thoughtless, uncouth Mozart, whose immortality will be as automatic as the process by which God "dictates" symphonies and operas to him. Not only in Salieri's eyes, but also in Shaffer's, Mozart is "the very voice of God." And his music is therefore perfect, timeless, "absolute."

The mystification of great art is itself a midcult precept—a central source of midcult's high tone and easy appeal. Correlating with Mozart's divinity, his "greatest" symphonies and concertos (like the greatest paintings and books) are sacred and remote. They exist on high, and also—significantly—far in the past. Their long familiarity makes them comforting. We do not think to interact with them in the here and now. We bask in their anodyne aura. Music itself, writes Shaffer in *Amadeus,* is "God's art."

Shaffer simplified these perceptions in "Paying Homage to Mozart," a September 2, 1984, *New York Times Magazine* article published in conjunction with the release of the *Amadeus* film. Music, he writes, is made "in heaven." Mozart is "the magic flute at the lips of God. . . . He died after a gigantic labor of sublime transcription." "Perfect," "faultless," Mozart's finest compositions "cannot be diminished by time." In fact, during the filming of *Amadeus,* the same Mozart pieces were played again and again. "Most music subjected to such treatment would soon outlive its welcome; yet everything we played of Mozart—no matter how often repeated—never staled or irritated, nor lost its power to enchant. . . . The music itself possesses the attributes of total invulnerability under the assault of relentless repetition. . . . I myself have found this mystery in Mozart to hold intact for almost 40 years." (How much more touching is Ferruccio Busoni's reflection in an August 2, 1906, letter to his wife: "All through [the] years the score of *Figaro* has remained unchanged in my estimation, like a lighthouse in surging seas. But when I looked at it again, a week ago, I discovered human weaknesses in it for the first time; and my soul flew for joy when I realized that I am not so far behind it as I thought, in spite of this discovery being a real loss, and pointing to the lack of durability in all human activities; [and how much more in my own!]")

Shaffer rejects talking "in vague, exalted terms about genius."

This is how he chooses to be concrete and specific: "The God I acknowledge lives, for example, in bars 34 to 44 of Mozart's Masonic Funeral Music." He rejects the "sentimental misjudgment" which has stereotyped Mozart as "charming but a little lightweight" and dismissed his church pieces as "secular and even frivolous." To Shaffer's taste, "the 46 bars of the *Ave Verum Corpus* contain more truly devotional feeling than the whole of *Parsifal*." He thinks the slow movement of Mozart's Clarinet Quintet "makes the rigorous turbulence of Beethoven seem overinsistent, and the lachrymose iterance of Mahler largely hysterical." Within Mozart's own output, he considers the Thirty-ninth Symphony "infinitely greater" than No. 40, and the finale of the *Jupiter* "one of the supreme achievements of art." He reluctantly finds that *Don Giovanni* suffers from a "disorganized and untheatrical libretto." *The Magic Flute,* however, "is almost too good for human beings."

So why is it, finally, that Mozart is great? As mystified by Shaffer, this is something one simply cannot talk about; great art, by its very definition, defies mortal analysis and comprehension.*

So what if *Amadeus* labels itself "art"—it's entertaining, isn't it? Ingesting the movie, I choked on its bathos and banality. The stage version, on Broadway, went down easier. Shaffer had fash-

---

*Anticipating Shaffer's mighty preference for a moment of Mozart to an evening of Wagner, the critic Lawrence Gilman once wrote: "We would rather hear Toscanini conduct a performance of the C major scale than hear Mr. Batonovich or Mr. Fortepiano conduct a performance of the First Symphony of Brahms." Challenged on this point by his colleague B. H. Haggin, Gilman amplified: "Some of us would rather hear Wanda Landowska play a single bar of Mozartean ornamentation than hear Mr. Poundergood play the whole of the D minor Concerto. We would rather hear Friedrich Schorr sing 'Das Ende! Das Ende!' in the second act of *Die Walküre* than hear the ordinary German baritone sing the entire role of Wotan." A Toscanini diehard, Gilman was a central figure in America's Toscanini cult until his death in 1939. Like Shaffer's, Gilman's midcult mentality combined populist principles and elevated metaphor. Like Shaffer appreciating Mozart, the Toscanini disciples (all of whom were also music appreciators) ranked composers and pieces

ioned a superb vehicle for Ian McKellen (a less self-conscious Salieri than H. Murray Abraham of the film). Conspiring against Mozart in flashbacks to vigorous middle age, McKellen's Salieri was an oily-smooth Machiavelli. Confiding to the audience ("ghosts of the future") as a visibly decrepit has-been, he was tormented by his conscience yet retained an intriguing, irredeemable wickedness.

McKellen's virtuosity proved a source of thoughtless pleasure, but only up to a point. This was because my thoughts, rather than accepting baited questions about the relationship of creativity to personality, fixed on quite different questions: about the relationship between *Amadeus* and its sources. Shaffer had said that his cartoon Mozart was not intended as a portrait of the real Amadeus. But that seemed disingenuous—if he had called his characters by other, unfamiliar names, the play would have forfeited its appeal. Furthermore, notwithstanding Shaffer's disclaimers, inferences of authenticity were inevitable. Grover Sales's album note for the original soundtrack recording of *Amadeus* (Fantasy Records) is a case in point:

> Shaffer draws an accurate though rarely seen picture of the gifted but childish composer based on exhaustive research into his life and music. . . .

---

in order of greatness. Olin Downes of the *New York Times* dismissed the *Pastorale* Symphony as a "work which for all its charm has never ranked among the great creations of Beethoven." Samuel Chotzinoff of the *New York Post* renumbered the Beethoven symphonies "in accordance with the true position of each on the spiritual scale." Haggin, in denigrating the Beethoven Violin Concerto as "comparatively feeble," recorded his "resentment" that Toscanini would devote himself "to anything less than the finest, the greatest music." This attitude of hortatory, contentious reverence bears pondering. It craves and coddles objects of worship. It denounces imposters and wards off agnostics. It is often encountered among adolescents and adult males. (Are women too socialized, insufficiently self-involved, to fetishize personal preferences so belligerently?) Consider, too, that prodigious discophiles are always men.

> [Mozart's gifts] lie beyond understanding, as though he
> had been a mutant. . . .
>
> [T]he portrait of Mozart handed down to us, tinged by
> Nineteenth Century romanticism, was that of a porcelain
> aesthete with heaven-cast eyes playing on a porcelain pi-
> ano. . . . *Amadeus* restores the actual Mozart as described
> by a host of his contemporaries, like the writer Karoline
> Pichler who witnessed him improvising on an aria from
> *Figaro* "so beautifully that everyone held his breath . . .
> but all at once he jumped up, and as he often did in his
> foolish moods, began to leap over table and chairs, miaow-
> ing like a cat, and turning somersaults like an unruly boy."

In fact, even as a cartoon, Shaffer's Mozart resembles no Mozart
I can glean. Mozart's letters, it is true, are artless and boyishly
irreverent; they also evoke a vigorous, inquisitive intelligence,
acutely perceptive of the human comedy. He was not the only
composer to turn somersaults in company; Wagner did it too
when he was excited. Mozart was not unique for breaking the spell
of some haunting improvisation with sudden foolishness; Beethoven would erupt into boisterous laughter and taunt his mesmer-
ized listeners. What is more, if Shaffer's cartoon Mozart contains
shreds of veracity, his Salieri and Joseph II are purely exploitative.
The former was no "musical idiot," restricted to "tonic and dominant, tonic and dominant," as Shaffer's Mozart claims. The latter
was no half-wit foil to Mozart's genius and Salieri's cunning; he
even showed musical talent. Salieri's quest for immortality, pow-
ering the play, is itself a convenient historical solecism; before
Beethoven, famous composers were not known to dwell on their
posthumous renown. Equally ahead of its time, in the *Amadeus*
movie, is Mozart's ostensible populism ("You belong here!" exclaims Shaffer's Emanuel Shickaneder, observing the triumph of
The Magic Flute in his theater). Finally, *Amadeus's* most insidious
misrepresentation is of itself as "art." Returning to Sales's album
note:

A "drama of ideas," . . . *Amadeus* probes universal themes that transcend both Mozart and Salieri. Foremost among these themes is the confrontation of mediocrity with genius, that nagging frustration common to all eras and pursuits. . . . Another theme is man's relation to God; how, as John Milton wondered, can God's often perverse and unjust ways be justified to man? Another theme of *Amadeus* that strikes a universal chord is the sad spectacle of a towering genius poorly rewarded by society. No more shocking or dramatic example in all of history can be found than Mozart.

Midcult, explained Macdonald, is perniciously ambiguous. Ostensibly raising mass culture, it razes high culture.

Ken Russell explores the possibilities of something better. The controversial director of such films as *Women in Love, The Devils, Tommy,* and *Altered States,* he is also our most prolific director of movies about famous composers—to date, his subjects have included Bartók, Debussy, Delius, Elgar, Liszt, Mahler, Richard Strauss, Tchaikovsky, and Vaughan Williams. While these films span a bewildering stylistic gamut, they all reject midcult.

Elgar, coming first (1962), is a quasi-documentary for the British Broadcasting Corporation. BBC canons stressed the use of archival footage of Elgar and his time. Where Russell employed actors, their faces could not be shown. And Russell was not permitted to write his own script. Nevertheless, the treatment of music is already special. Russell applies the famous First "Pomp and Circumstance" March ironically, in parallel with the composer's own later perception of Empire jaded and diminished: we hear it as a backdrop to footage of blind soldiers in procession, hands on one another's shoulders, eyes bandaged shut.

Russell's Delius film of 1968, *Song of Summer,* was his first full-length treatment of a composer. Though another BBC production, it allowed him the creative license of a film biography. Max

Adrian's performance is a tour de force. As the blind Delius, dictating music to his amanuensis, Eric Fenby, Adrian achieves an uncanny visualization of the creative act. *The Music Lovers,* Russell's 1970 Tchaikovsky film, leaves television behind; a United Artists feature, it is typically, daringly subjective (the opening title reads in full: "Ken Russell's film on Tchaikovsky and The Music Lovers"). Abandoning the verisimilitude of *Song of Summer, The Music Lovers* distorts, fantasizes, and reinvents. To an even greater degree, this is the method of Russell's subsequent feature-length composer films. *Mahler* (1974) and *Lisztomania* (1975) are progressively more schematic, more stylized. Roger Daltry, as Liszt, is a rock star. His scheming colleague Wagner is a vampire.

To Peter Shaffer, in *Amadeus,* creativity is inexplicable—for the purposes of analysis, a dead end. To Russell it is a starting point. Like Shaffer, he eschews film biography. But whereas Shaffer selects and shapes Mozart materials to heighten his plot and extract his thesis, Russell seizes incidents and environments likely to illuminate the relationship of art to artist. Specifically, Russell is obsessed with the personal origins of music, a hidden dimension encompassing both external circumstance and interior experience. Like a great choreographer—like Balanchine, inferring latent possibilities for movement and gesture in Stravinsky or Tchaikovsky—he "materializes" music, his imprint so finely felt that what we see deepens our engagement in what we hear. *The Music Lovers* documents Russell's power to "see" music; set beside *Amadeus,* it also clarifies the achievements of Shaffer and Forman.

Russell's view of Tchaikovsky's harried life and personality is trenchant but standard. Maladjusted, histrionic, Tchaikovsky confuses fantasy and reality. He never recovers from the early loss of his mother. Neurotically attached to his siblings, he likens his sister to an angel. This hothouse family milieu arrests his emotional and sexual development. His homosexuality makes him feel scorned and inadequate. His voluminous thirteen-year correspondence with Mme. von Meck, whom he resolves never to meet, is a surrogate relationship confirming his limitations. Even more pathetic is his brief and disastrous marriage to Antonina Milyukova: attempting to appear "normal" to himself and others, he falls apart. He ends his life by drinking water contaminated with cholera, the same disease that killed his mother.

Melvyn Bragg's screenplay (based largely on Tchaikovsky's extensive correspondence) is a straightforward, even rudimentary exegesis of this interpretation. The compressed, unnatural dialogue imparts information unceremoniously; little attempt is made to simulate the pace and texture of real life. The physical production, too, is unprepossessing; compared to Forman's painstaking creation of Mozart's Vienna (filmed in Prague), Russell creates a cut-and-paste Moscow. With the exception of Glenda Jackson's portrait of the demented Antonina, Russell's actors are not notably subtle. Richard Chamberlain, in the central role, is a strong presence, but undetailed; Tchaikovsky's nervous sensitivity, his chronic shyness and fits of depression, are barely limned. And Chamberlain does not look the part; compared to H. Murray Abraham's sensational "aging," as Salieri, Chamberlain fails even to grow properly wrinkled and worn. Superficially, *The Music Lovers* is as careless and unsophisticated as *Amadeus* is polished. Its power is interior.

The principal source of this power is Tchaikovsky's music. Only Stanley Kubrick, among major contemporary filmmakers, treats music with something like the respect and understanding Russell accords it here. To begin with, there is the visual integrity of the scenes of music in performance. Quite obviously, Chamberlain is himself a pianist. Even though it is not he, but Rafael Orozco, who performs the B-flat minor Piano Concerto on the soundtrack, Chamberlain is the most convincing pianist-mime in the history of the cinema: his stentorian chords, his octave cascades, his streaking arpeggios are not only perfectly synchronized with Orozco's; his every gesture of arms and torso tells. Significantly, music is the one area where Russell insists on verisimilitude; in the *Amadeus* film, the "conducting"—of H. Murray Abraham and of Tom Hulce as Mozart—is farcical by comparison. In contrast to

Joseph II's stupid and implausible putdown of *The Abduction from the Seraglio* in *Amadeus* ("too many notes"), Nicholas Rubinstein's notorious repudiation of the B-flat minor Concerto is taken seriously by Russell and Bragg ("it's not only trivial, it's bad, vulgar"—a remark illustrated at the keyboard with passages from the concerto that *are* vulgar). And—unlike Shaffer and Forman—Russell does not mutilate music: all the big Tchaikovsky extracts possess a beginning and an end. In fact, they are typically foregrounded—predicating the action, supplanting the dialogue.

And so the opening scene of *The Music Lovers,* lasting four minutes, is a Ken Russell ballet: Moscow's Shrovetide carnival. The ballet (no one speaks) comprises a series of tableaus introducing and characterizing the neurotic dramatis personae: Tchaikovsky and his lover, Chiluvsky, cavort with children on a slide. The future Nina Tchaikovsky eyes a handsome soldier, whom she pelts with a snowball. The self-obsessed Mme. von Meck turns her back on the festivities. Tchaikovsky's brother Modeste winces with distaste. Equally out of place is their sister, Sasha, an anxious passerby on her husband's arm. Tchaikovsky turns to follow her, but is pulled away by Chiluvsky. Foreshadowing Tchaikovsky's story, the scene is blatantly fanciful. Yet the music, with its high spirits and hurtling trajectory, binds it and also helps establish an aesthetic that shuns naturalism as surely as Tchaikovsky's escapist life-style shuns nature.

The film's second set piece is the premiere of the B-flat minor Concerto at the Moscow Conservatory. In real life, the pianist was Hans von Bülow and the performance took place in Boston; Russell has Tchaikovsky at the keyboard and situates Chiluvsky, Nina, Mme. von Meck, Modeste, and Sasha in the auditorium, each playing a part. There are twelve minutes of music, uninterrupted by dialogue. The opening of the first movement is heard (mm. 1–54), after which Russell breaks away to show Mme. von Meck's late arrival outside the hall. When the music resumes (as she enters her box), the movement is near its close (m. 640). The second movement is given complete—after which Tchaikovsky, from whose perspective we are now listening, is lost in thought even while performing. He regains "consciousness" near the close of the finale (the orchestral buildup just before the soloist's final octave barrage at m. 174)—at which point the music fades in and continues to the concerto's close.

Russell's visualization of the tripartite second movement is elaborate. As experienced by Tchaikovsky the pianist, the outer sections (*andantino semplice*) evoke an incestuous pastoral with Tchaikovsky and Sasha. The central *prestissimo* depicts a love affair that Nina, in the audience, fantasizes sharing with the Shrovetide soldier. The sibling idyll, amid sunlit trees and water, is a telling but perilously obvious application of the music's ephemeral reverie. Russell undermines sentimentality by doubling the cliché: Tchaikovsky and Sasha race through the woods in slow motion—a parody of the Hollywood/Madison Avenue convention. The result is amusingly absurd, yet paradoxically protects (and touchingly projects) the innocence of Tchaikovsky the composer. Nina's fantasy is a tour de force: the synchronization of musical and dramatic gesture is beyond praise. Where the violas and cellos strike up a giggly music-hall tune accompanied by rhythmic bursts of sixteenth notes in the piano (m. 72), Russell sees a pair of galloping horses. A wider shot reveals an open white carriage whose swift, smooth perpetual motion is musical. Its occupants are Nina and the soldier, laughing and embracing. With the reprise of the *prestissimo*'s first idea (m. 125), the lovers chase one another into the woods. The fantasy accelerates; Nina and the soldier marry. A sharp orchestral exclamation (m. 132) shatters her daydream: suddenly, Nina is seated at Tchaikovsky's concert. The piano's falling cascades match her puzzled, then disappointed, descent to terra firma.

In other words, Russell's method is to *begin* with the music, never to apply it as an afterthought. It is the main course, not the condiment. He savors it, comments on it, even criticizes it. When the B-flat minor Concerto's blatant opening makes Rubinstein, in the audience, wince with discomfort, we side with Rubinstein, not Tchaikovsky. Russell apparently prefers the Third Symphony's exquisite *andante elegiaco;* it inspires a glimpse of Tchaikovsky in bed, alongside the disconsolate Nina, despairing of his impotence. The music eschews outburst; and Tchaikovsky's sobbing, as depicted by Russell, is not extravagant but a quiet, private expression of loneliness, of thwarted personal need.

This Tchaikovsky mode finds its most explicit, most telling expression—as unfulfilled sexual arousal—in the person of Tatyana, in *Eugene Onegin.* Her hopeless tender passion, with which the composer (by his own admission) identified, is the topic of her letter scene. In *The Music Lovers,* Tchaikovsky composes the letter scene yearning for the unattainable Sasha (he even tells her: "It's you I think of when I write the music"). And it is the letter scene aria, as well, to which Nina writes Tchaikovsky her letter of ardent supplication. Confusing Nina, Sasha, and Tatyana, Russell's Tchaikovsky sets eyes on Nina but does not see her. Mme. von Meck's correspondence, too, finds its way into Russell's elaborate letter scene sequence—for this is another necessarily idealized, vicarious, unconsummated relationship. In themselves, the analogies are simplistic. But the music—its pathetic hopefulness, its yearning for intimacy—penetrates.

The condition of expectant, unfulfillable sexuality is quintessential Tchaikovsky. Its quintessential complement, escaping adult pain, is a world of fairy-tale artifice and illusion: the lost innocence of *Swan Lake, Sleeping Beauty,* and *The Nutcracker.* Russell has Tchaikovsky and Nina encounter *Swan Lake* in outdoor performance on their honeymoon. But even here, the psychologically shackled Tchaikovsky cannot escape. Nina, as ever, is uncomprehending. Chiluvsky, who happens to be present, explains to her: "The man is the prince, the woman is called Odile. He thinks she's the pure beautiful swan whom he thinks of marrying. But she's a cheat. She'll destroy him. . . . Do you know what she's saying? She's saying 'You and your ideal love will die.'" Tchaikovsky himself, who overhears this jealous exegesis, looks at Odette and sees Sasha. As dialogue, the writing is merely pat. As background to the ballet, it unobtrusively urges a personalized response. Even the overcast weather—it has been raining—is superbly conducive to a meaningful experience of the music.

The emotional climax of *The Music Lovers*—the film's central pièce de résistance—is a four-minute scene trapping Tchaikovsky and his bride in a railroad carriage. Its inspiration, from Tchaikovsky's letters, is threefold: that Tchaikovsky instantly found Nina "totally repugnant" physically; that he "fell into deep despair" and began "passionately, avidly longing for death"; and that on the bridal night he traveled with her, by train, to St. Petersburg, a journey that began with him "ready to cry out with choking sobs." Fortunately, at the second stop Tchaikovsky encountered an old friend, in whom he could privately confide in "a flood of tears." This calmed him down so that the remainder of the trip "was not particularly awful."

In Russell's version the journey is from St. Petersburg to Moscow, and there is no friend. The train jolts to and fro; the cramped compartment's gas lamp sways violently, luridly illuminating the unhappy couple with sudden shafts of brightness. Sweating and dishevelled, Tchaikovsky and Nina guzzle champagne. He is fully clothed; her breasts are bare. She kisses him passionately; he freezes. She removes her corset and falls onto the floor, writhing on her back; he is terrified of her nakedness. Russell's cameras, always tight, panning tighter, scrutinize the newlyweds from every angle of the tiny room. The soundtrack (no words are spoken) consists of the first movement of the *Pathétique* Symphony—the central calamity (*sempre dolente ed appassionato*) of the development section (mm. 171–97, 262–99)—elided with the triple-*forte* coda of the *Manfred* Symphony (from m. 291), movement 1. The *Pathétique* cries suicide. The *Manfred* music, through its use earlier in the film, evokes Tchaikovsky's memory of his beloved mother in her death throes: naked, hideously writhing (as Nina is now), she is lifted into a bathtub—the "water cure" for cholera—in which she expires. The claustrophobia of the dark, jolting compartment; the dilemma of its occupants; the music's relentless wailing and pounding—all this creates aural and visual impressions of unbearable discomfort. The juxtaposition of image and music, moreover, is grating rather than smooth: the avalanche of the *Pathétique* climax contradicts the train's jerky rhythm. The scene is debilitating for its intensity, funny for its extravagance. If we enjoy it, we feel guilty; if we don't, we are prudes. At the same time, Russell has employed Tchaikovsky's music with devastating honesty. Rather than illustrating the agony of the *Pathétique* Symphony by showing its composer eyeing a vial of poison, he produces a wife whose sexual arousal disgusts and horrifies her husband—a wife he has acquired to prove to himself and the world that he is respectable. The desperation of Tchaikovsky the man, Russell tells us, activates the despairing *Pathétique.* Its romantic anguish transcends cliché. Russell has discovered a visual image for Tchaikovsky's music that is startling, stimulating, ingeniously apt.

The Music Lovers was lambasted by unsympathetic film critics. But even those who reject it as trash cannot come away from the film rejecting Tchaikovsky as trash. Without saying so in words, Russell confutes the view that Tchaikovsky is sentimental. Without preaching or boasting, he celebrates the emotional veracity of Tchaikovsky the composer.

Like *The Music Lovers, Amadeus* incorporates the music of its composer protagonist—and treats it as trivially as every other aspect of the Mozart story. Onstage, *Amadeus* administers its music in small doses. Onscreen, the doses are larger and more frequent.

A key musical excerpt, occurring moments after Salieri first encounters Mozart in the palace of Archbishop Colloredo, samples the slow movement of the B-flat Wind Serenade, K. 361. Salieri is hiding behind a table, watching Mozart tease his wife-to-be with obscene word games. Suddenly, Mozart hears the opening strains of K. 361, leaps up, and rushes off to conduct the assembled players. This performance consists of measures 1–9 of the *adagio* glued to the final thirty-one measures of the concluding rondo. Salieri watches in disbelief, then tells us: "That was Mozart! That giggling, dirty-minded creature I'd just seen crawling on the floor!" Then he examines the score and reports: "On the page it looked—nothing! The beginning simple, almost comic. Just a pulse: bassoons, bassett horns—like a rusty squeeze box. And then, high above it, an oboe—a single note—hanging there unwavering—until a clarinet took it over and sweetened it into a phrase of such delight! This was no composition by a performing monkey! This was a music I'd never heard—filled with such longing, such unfulfillable longing, it seemed to me that I was hearing the voice of God! But why—why would God choose an obscene child to be his instrument?"

Salieri tells us what to think of K. 361. Even by midcult standards, this prose description of great art, superimposed on the music it narrates, is leaden. More informative is what the music itself tells us to think—in particular, the cut from an *adagio* E-flat major cadence to a brisk B-flat major coda. With this unmusical gesture, we are told to regard Mozart's B-flat Wind Serenade as an accompaniment to an anecdote.

In his 1984 *New York Times Magazine* article, Shaffer writes: "In the picture, the music naturally became more prominent than in the play. This is not just because on screen one can show operas that can only be described on stage. The paradox is that in a live theater one cannot successfully play long stretches of music without subverting the drama and turning the event into a concert, whereas the cinema positively *welcomes* music in floods." But "floods of music" is Russell's method, never Shaffer's. If *Amadeus* floods us, it is with accumulated trickles: a little K. 183, then some K. 201, a smattering of K. 365, K. 364, K. 482 . . . the soundtrack becomes a Mozart smorgasbord in which all the food blandly intermingles on a single huge, sloppy platter. This is because the film's frequent musical usage is not (as with the B-flat Serenade) merely ancillary, but also careless and nonspecific. Take, for instance, the *Kyrie* from the C minor Mass, of which we hear the opening seventy seconds. This is applied to a narrative episode: Leopold Mozart appeals to Colloredo to reconsider banishing Mozart from his court. Colloredo agrees. Leopold kisses his hand and departs; the voice-over narration is from a subsequent letter to Wolfgang: "I am coming to Vienna. Take no further steps towards marriage till we meet." Cut to Wolfgang's marriage to Constanze Weber, in a fine cathedral. The priest intones: "I now join you in the holy bonds of matrimony. Those whom God has joined together let no man put asunder." Cut to Leopold Mozart reading a letter from his son: Wolfgang intends to "conquer Vienna" with his new wife. Leopold angrily crumples the letter; the music abruptly stops.

Granted, this stern C minor *Kyrie* conveys something of Leopold's disposition; and its religious aura resonates with Colloredo and with the marriage ceremony. But it is hardly marriage music. As letter-reading music, its appropriation is parasitic: it strengthens a stranded vignette by binding it to the preceding material. The priest's superfluous words (the ceremony would play perfectly without them) likewise act to neutralize and subordinate the music.

Other than five minutes from the slow movement of the D minor Piano Concerto, which accompanies the closing credits, only one musical extract is heard at any length during the *Amadeus* film. This comprises five and one-half minutes from the penultimate scene of *Don Giovanni,* in which the statue of the dead Commendatore comes to dinner. We see Constanze inform Wolfgang: "Your father is dead." Cut to Leopold's portrait on the wall; on the soundtrack: the first awesome D minor chord announcing the Commendatore's visit. With chord number two (the dominant A major, in its first inversion), we are watching the Commendatore onstage, in performance, crashing through a wall into Don Giovanni's dining room. Excepting a single excision, the great scene, execrably dubbed, is played out to its conclusion. Leporello trembles in fear of his life. The statue refuses mortal food and summons Don Giovanni to dine with him. The Don manfully accepts. He grips the statue's hand; his body freezes. "Repent!" cries the statue. "No, obstinate old man!" Aswirl with demons, the room collapses. Don Giovanni descends to hell.

We are already watching and hearing, in sung performance, the most terrifying pages from any Mozart stage work. But, over the music, Salieri must tell us what we have already figured out: "So rose the dreadful ghost from his next and blackest opera. There on the stage stood the figure of a dead Commander calling. And I know—only I understand—that the horrifying apparition was Leopold raised from the dead. . . . Wolfgang had actually summoned up his own father to accuse his son, before all the world— it was terrifying and wonderful to watch." As the statue descends a staircase toward Don Giovanni, Forman's cameras cut to Salieri, watching from a box, to Mozart, conducting in the pit, to the aged Salieri, who supplies this painstaking narrative. Back onstage, Don Giovanni's harried exchange with the statue escalates ("Parlo, ascolta! più tempo non ho!"). Salieri, commandeering Shaffer's plot, continues: "And now . . . the madness began in me—the madness, the madness splitting in half. Through my influence I saw to it *Don Giovanni* was played only five times in Vienna. But in secret I went to every one of those five, worshipping sound I alone seemed to hear." We are now at the crucial moment where the statue pronounces Giovanni damned. Salieri resumes: "And as I stood there I understood how that bitter old man was still possessing his poor son even from beyond the grave—I began to see a way, a terrible way, I could finally triumph over God." But, in league with Forman and Shaffer, Salieri has killed Mozart already. Their busy interventions ensure that he is too feeble to stand alone.

Russell, as we have seen, applies the coda of *Manfred*'s first movement to the death of Tchaikovsky's naked, writhing mother—so that its recurrence when the adult Tchaikovsky is confronted by a naked woman is interpretive. In the *Amadeus* film, the two great tonic and dominant chords beginning the overture—and, later, announcing the statue—symbolize both Mozart's father and the black-robed, black-masked messenger who commissions the requiem. (Unbeknownst to Mozart, he is sent by Salieri, who plans to pass off this music as his own at Mozart's funeral.) Russell's *Manfred* leitmotif, used twice, is almost subliminal—we may become consciously aware of it only with a second or third viewing. Forman's *Don Giovanni* leitmotif intrudes five times with such rudeness that we get the idea long before it is done getting us. The movie begins with the Commendatore's chords; they punctuate Salieri's offscreen cries: "Mozart! Mozart! Forgive your assassin!" Later, when Mozart is striding home while "composing" the finale of the K. 450 piano concerto in his head, he opens the door to find his looming, black-robed father, arriving from Salzburg. The concerto extract cadences on B-flat; the statue's first, D minor chord illiterately intrudes; Wolfgang exclaims: "Papa!" The third occurrence, initiating the *Don Giovanni* extract described above, is when Constanze says "Your father is dead." The fourth, brutally interrupting the composition of the D minor Piano Concerto, is the stranger's first visit: when Mozart opens the door and sees the masked messenger, the restlessly pulsating concerto segues, *attacca,* to the statue's massive chordal knell; "Herr Mozart?" the messenger blandly inquires. "I have come to commission a work from you." The final occurrence is the messenger's second visit. This time Mozart is dancing to the *Magic Flute* Overture coursing through his brain when the loud knocking begins. He opens the door, we see the stern black mask, and the cruel *Don Giovanni* chords silence the cheerful *Magic Flute.* This is already a Monty Python skit. Every divine morsel of meaning comes delivered on a silver plate. Spoonfed the pabulum of reverence, we decline even to chew.

Would only a snob reject *Amadeus?* Impossible—because, more than any Mozart opera, *Amadeus* is itself a snobbish entertainment. And this, finally, is what unmasks its every important-sounding message and messenger. Salieri's pretentious explanations narrow our understanding of Mozart and his music. Clement Greenberg, in a famous assault on kitsch, wrote: "[It] predigests art for the spectator and spares him effort, provides him with a shortcut to the pleasure of arts." Macdonald, inveighing against kitsch as an attribute of midcult, wrote: "It does its feeling for [us]." Shaffer, as Salieri, offers a shortcut to Mozart that becomes a detour. Russell, less a snob, offers no shortcuts; by letting the music explain the composer, he broadens our receptivity. Shaffer's revisionism is phony: appropriating one myth (Salieri the poisoner) and creating another (Mozart the idiot), he teaches nothing. Russell, who never pontificates, debunks the myth that Tchaikovsky is shallow.

"Eternal," "divine," "miraculous," "unique," "incomparable," "faultless," "profound," "supreme," "timeless," "sublime," "perfect," Mozart à la Shaffer disarms critical understanding; slavishly enfeebled by *Amadeus,* we humbly decline the prerogatives of exploratory engagement. Challenging, even antagonizing accustomed channels of feeling and perception, *The Music Lovers* inculcates curiosity. This is what is supposed to happen in high culture. But *The Music Lovers* is not high culture; nor, unlike *Amadeus,* does it purport to be. Rather, camp is Russell's technique for encompassing the extravagance of Tchaikovsky and his music, for counteracting the clichés of romantic suffering and angst. Camp, as Susan Sontag says in her "Notes on Camp," is "high-spirited" and "unpretentious":

> One is drawn to Camp when one realizes that "sincerity" is not enough. Sincerity can be simple philistinism, intellectual narrowness. . . . The traditional means for going beyond straight seriousness—irony, satire—seem feeble today, inadequate to the culturally oversaturated medium in which contemporary sensibility is schooled. Camp introduces a new standard: artifice as an ideal, theatricality.

Russell's mélange of highbrow and low is peculiarly contemporary. It also happens to parallel the polyvalence of *Don Giovanni,* which Mozart called a "serious comedy," and of *The Magic Flute,* whose dual appeal to aesthete and groundling recalls Shakespeare. Characterizing his first three piano concertos for Vienna (K. 413, 414, and 415), Mozart himself wrote: "These concertos are a happy medium between what is too easy and too difficult. . . . There are passages here and there from which connoisseurs alone can derive satisfaction; but these passages were written in such a way that the less learned cannot fail to be pleased, though without knowing why."

(1992)

2 · *Of Swimming and Dancing*

On Staging Wagner's *Ring*

In his compendium *Nietzsche Contra Wagner,* Friedrich Nietzsche characterized Wagner as a "danger":

> One walks into the sea, gradually loses one's secure footing, and finally surrenders oneself to the elements without reservation: one must *swim.* In older music, what one had to do . . . was something quite different, namely, to *dance.* The measure required for this, the maintenance of certain equally balanced units of time and force, demanded continual *wariness* for the listener's soul—and on the counterplay of this cooler breeze rests the magic of all *good* music. Richard Wagner wanted a different kind of movement; he overthrew the physiological presupposition of previous music. Swimming, floating—no longer walking and dancing.

Though Nietzsche's condemnation of "swimming" specifically rejects Wagner's "endless melody," it powerfully summarizes other elements of his ongoing Wagner critique as well. Wagner's own, inconsistent view of what his music did to people partook of Schopenhauer, for whom music embodied "feeling" and "passion," not "reason." Far removed from "all reflection and conscious intention," music, in Schopenhauer's view, spoke "a language that [the composer's] reasoning faculty does not understand, just as a magnetic somnambulist gives information about things of which she has no conception when she is awake."

The notion of Wagner incapacitating the mind, crippling the conscious, autonomous will to act, is Nietzsche's notion of Wagner as a drug, narcotic, intoxicant. Like the water of Nietzsche's metaphor, or the trance of Schopenhauer's somnambulist, he subverts self-control. Fixated on subconscious, often erotic subject matter, he activates forbidden impulses.

Twentieth-century aesthetic and political currents have more amplified than silenced Nietzsche's critique. Thomas Mann—like Nietzsche, infatuated with Wagner as a young man, and incurably ambivalent afterward—is a bellwether. In a 1935 letter, Mann found himself

> more and more . . . an Apollonian, while the Dionysian appeals to me less and less. Just consider Richard Wagner as an intellectual and a human being. Confused, helpless, and at a loss, full of longing in every direction, longing for life and longing for death—dreadful, when you think about it. . . . Have you ever read anything by him that showed him as an intellectual lord and master of life? It is not fair to think of Goethe. But I can't help thinking of him, because he has reason as mankind's crowning glory.

Five years later, by which time Europe was at war and Mann was living in the United States, Wagner's unbridled "feeling" and "passion" component seemed indissolubly linked with Third Reich Germany. Mann now wrote:

> [Wagner's] work, created and directed "against civilization," against the entire culture and society dominant since the Renaissance, emerges from the bourgeois-humanist epoch in the same manner as does Hitlerism.

With its *Wagalaweia* and its alliteration, its mixture of roots-in-the-soil and eyes-toward-the-future, its appeal for a classless society, its mythical-reactionary revolutionism—with all these, it is the exact spiritual forerunner of the "metapolitical" movement today terrorizing the world.

After the war, in a 1949 letter, Mann wrote: "There is, in Wagner's bragging, his endless holding-forth, his passion for monologue, his insistence on having a say in everything, an unspeakable arrogance that prefigures Hitler—oh, yes, there's a good deal of 'Hitler' in Wagner."

A good deal, and—from other perspectives, equally well known to Mann—not so much; the same letter finds him breathlessly extolling *Lohengrin's* "silvery-blue beauty" and closing: "How the subject of Wagner rejuvenates me!" In the postwar decades, Wagner has gradually—but never fully—recuperated from the Hitler association. Conflicted Wagnerians continue to grapple with Nietzschean accusations of narcosis. In *The New Grove Wagner,* Carl Dahlhaus propounds a Wagner aesthetic of feeling plus reason, floating plus walking:

> Undoubtedly Wagner's music, like all Romantic art, seeks to "transport" the listener; but being "beside one's self" . . . does not exclude by any means . . . "circumspection." . . . The "associative magic" [of leitmotifs] of which Thomas Mann speaks is magic, certainly, but one that instead of paralyzing the spellbound listener challenges him to use his mind to make the associations; and the Dionysian intoxication described by Nietzsche in *Die Geburt der Tragödie* is not the negation of Apollonian contemplation but leads on to it. The blind frenzy in which enthusiasm for Wagner has sometimes lost itself is as inadequate a response to his work as . . . pedantry.

Wagner so richly embodies the cultural ferment of his time, so complexly resonates with timeless themes, that our changing attitudes toward his operas can seem as fascinating as the operas themselves. And all of this—the man, his work, the thoughts and feelings engendered—is further illuminated by the evolving history of Wagner in performance: a history encapsulated at the House of Wagner itself. It was at Bayreuth that the Wagner-equals-Hitler equation was pursued to the hilt: Winifred Wagner, Bayreuth's director from 1931 to 1944, was Hitler's friend; the Führer favored her festival with his swastikas, his patronage, and his frequent presence. And it was at Bayreuth, too, that his evil spell—the disproportionate stress on Wagner's racism and unsavory nationalism that he and his followers promoted—was notably expunged. With the reopening of the festival in 1951, Wagner's grandsons Wieland and Wolfgang promulgated a new philosophy of staging: instead of worshipful "fidelity" to the Master, ceaseless reevaluation. Discarding the literalism of horses and winged helmets, Wieland—the festival's reigning artistic intelligence until his death in 1966—darkened the stage, minimized movement, and stripped scenery, props, and costumes to essentials. Cyclorama projections suggested mood and place. Transcultural symbolism supplanted Teutonic nationalism.

For two decades, the "New Bayreuth" style seemed ubiquitous; imitations turned up everywhere. In retrospect, New Bayreuth was but one stage in the overthrow of romantic, "swimming" Wagner, with its pernicious political implications and musty physical trappings; a more thorough unraveling of Old Bayreuth, fortified by a more complete investigation of Nietzschean dancing and walking, was inevitable. After Wieland's initiative, one took Wagner seriously by subverting him.

There followed a Bayreuth staging that provoked more consternation than Wieland's stagings ever did: Götz Friedrich's *Tannhäuser,* new in 1972. More than Wieland, Friedrich, a Walter Felsenstein disciple, refused to accept Wagner on his own terms. Unlike Wieland's, his symbols fostered didactic demystification, not ambiguous myth. By New Bayreuth standards, he flooded the stage with light, movement, gesture. Interpreting an opera itself about swimming versus walking, feeling versus thinking, he heightened the dialectic of Tannhäuser's indecisiveness by shocking the Bayreuth audience into mental arousal. The Landgraf became a fascist despot who rode to the hunt in a sedan chair, and whose courtiers saluted Nazi-style. The final tableau admitted no flowered staff, no redemption, no swimming catharsis. If this seemed irresolute, it exposed Wagner's own vagueness and irresolution—an insight shrewdly underlined by Dahlhaus, in *The New Grove Wagner:*

> All Wagner's works, from *Der fliegende Holländer* to *Parsifal,* returned to the idea of "redemption": The truly fundamental dramatic motive, with which any interpretation must begin, is not, however, the redemption that Wagner sought and longed for but the entanglement that he felt reality to be. Reality was oppressive and painful, and the sense of being trapped in it was the fundamental emotion that made a dramatic, rather than a lyric or an epic, creative artist of him. In Wagner's work—the prose as well as the dramas—redemption is always precarious and under threat . . . there is hardly an ending in his dramas that is not ambivalent. The endings always provided his biggest dramaturgical problem, and the fact that he changed them (*Tannhäuser*), left them open to interpretation (the *Ring*), considered and then rejected modification (*Lohengrin*), meddled with the musical style (which is a dramaturgical factor: *Der fliegende Holländer*), or sought refuge in cryptic formula (*Parsifal*) is one of the characteristics of his creative process.

Friedrich's heresies set the stage for the Bayreuth centenary *Ring* of 1976: Patrice Chéreau's memorable concatenation of realism and symbolism, whimsy and analysis, charm and belligerence.

Like Friedrich's, Chéreau's work bristled with animated, realistically detailed acting. Like Friedrich's, its contemporaneity implicitly rejected redemption-through-love. But Chéreau's playfulness made his *Ring* more buoyant than Friedrich's *Tannhäuser* lesson, and Richard Peduzzi's stage pictures, coolly colored and lit, evoked the detached sensibility of a René Magritte or Robert Wilson. To the intellectually fashionable, the Chéreau *Ring* looked postmodern, and his way of second-guessing Wagner was deconstructive. In particular, Chéreau scaled down or contradicted the cycle's numerous heroic speeches and deeds beginning with those of Wotan, whose scowling face, stalking gait, and grasping gestures layered his "noblest" utterances with duplicity. Among other things, Chéreau's critique suggested an exposé of the *Ring* itself, of the alleged arrogance and fulsome rhetoric of its creator; he even dressed Wotan as Wagner. Concomitantly, Siegfried's heroic speeches emerged as naive delusions. The production's blasphemies arose logically from this revisionist scenario, in which Wotan's power lust, reconsidered, overthrew Wagner's contradictory case for Siegfried's guileless self-knowledge and manipulable free-agency. Fafner the dragon motored on four large wheels: He was a Siegfried toy supplied by Wotan. The Forest Bird was another of Wotan's crafty props, caged to stay put until Siegfried managed to find it. Siegfried didn't forge Nothung—a Wotan-supplied machine manufactured it for him. Too weak to budge Fafner's corpse, Siegfried petulantly kicked it. Aroused by Brünnhilde, he fell on his back and kicked his heels. Especially as complemented by Pierre Boulez's blasphemous conducting—light-footed, precise, emptied of angst and erotic turmoil—Chéreau's *Ring* "danced." It compelled "continual wariness." It exuded a "cooler breeze."

Heterodox Chéreau-style "dancing" Wagner subsequently pervaded Europe, supplanting stark, dark New Bayreuth–style stagings. Meanwhile, at New York's Metropolitan Opera, the closest thing to something new was something old: its 1977 *Tannhäuser*, directed by Otto Schenk and designed by Günther Schneider-

Siemssen in a manner as Romantic and naturalistic as Wagner's own stage aesthetic. As a leading Bayreuth singer remarked to me in 1978, the Met's purposely old-fashioned *Tannhäuser* would have been "impossible in Europe"; in New York, it triumphed. The Met subsequently prevailed on Schenk and Schneider-Siemssen to supply a *Die Walküre*—the initial component in a new *Ring*—with recognizable rocks and trees, and a first-act living room complete with roof, walls, and a hearth. The same year—1986—the Seattle Opera presented a new *Ring* staged by François Rochaix with sets and costumes by Robert Israel. Rather than swimming in a purgative bath of heroic rage and compassion, the Met *Walküre* sank under the dead weight of purported "tradition"; Seattle's *Ring,* in which postmodern and deconstructive elements coexisted with a rendering of character and plot more faithful than Chéreau's, swam and danced, stirred the heart, tickled the brain.

Though summer *Ring* cycles have been a Seattle tradition since 1975, previous Seattle *Ring*s were, by all accounts, theatrically undistinguished: the rocks were styrofoam; the singers wore corny bearskins, breastplates, and horned helmets; no special effort was made to forge an integrated whole. The present *Ring* is the brainchild of Speight Jenkins, who took over the company in 1982. Jenkins is an ardent Wagnerian for whom mounting the *Ring* was a labor of love, a dream come true. His first move was to talk Wagner with Robert Israel, whose work in Minnesota and Europe he had heard about, and whose sets and costumes for Philip Glass's *Satyagraha* he had seen at the Brooklyn Academy of Music. Jenkins admired Israel's "feeling for ritual and fantasy"; he "felt very strongly Israel was the man to do the Seattle *Ring.*" Rochaix, a stage and opera director from Geneva, was suggested to Jenkins by the conductor Jeffrey Tate. Israel and Rochaix met in Geneva and "clicked"—at the time, neither had undertaken any Wagner. Seattle's summer 1985 *Walküre,* in which they were joined by the lighting designer Joan Sullivan, was their first collaboration. The full *Ring* followed a summer later.

Like Chéreau and countless other post-Wieland *Ring* masters, Rochaix updates the story: Israel's sets and costumes usually evoke Wagner's own nineteenth century. At the same time, Seattle's is not a realistic *Ring*. *Das Rheingold's* underwater opening is played on a stage draped in billowing blue taffeta; the Rhinemaidens wear Victorian bloomers (the first of many reminders of Jacques Schmidt's costumes for Chéreau). In scene 2, a simple wooden platform-and-stairs leads upward toward invisible Valhalla; Wotan is dressed as Wagner, and Fricka wears a bustle. Nibelheim's lanterns and flashing lights evoke a mine; the Nibelungen are exploited child laborers. In *Siegfried,* act 1, Siegfried enters leading an actual bear cub. Rather than real horses, however, the Valkyries ride airborne carousel steeds manipulated by wires.

Like Chéreau, Rochaix second-guesses both Wotan and Wagner. To this end, he makes Wotan-Wagner the central actor in a play he himself directs. The set for *Die Walküre,* act 2, for instance, features a wooden assemblage of stairs and platforms thirty-two feet high; when rotated (by eight visible stagehands), it proves to be the backside of a prop: the tower from which Brünnhilde announces Siegmund's death. The Wotan-Fricka and Wotan-Brünnhilde exchanges, in other words, take place "backstage"; Wotan's play is the one about Siegmund and Sieglinde. As in Chéreau, Wotan's mania for control is stressed. So is Siegfried's dependence: as in Chéreau, the Forest Bird is an inanimate prop, a toy on a stick. But Rochaix's Siegfried really forges his sword. Later, in the process of killing Fafner, he knocks over the flimsy painted flats constituting Wotan's "forest." This assertion of autonomy brings him into line with Wagner's intended Siegfried and enables Wotan to achieve his intended resignation and wisdom.

To underline Siegfried's coming of age, Rochaix inserts a touching pantomime into *Siegfried,* act 3, just after Siegfried penetrates the Magic Fire: he envisions his father's murder, his mother's death in childbirth, Fafner's warning, and the Forest Bird's summons. Fortified by new self-knowledge, he tentatively kisses

Brünnhilde. Rochaix's handling of this long final scene is so honest that for once Siegfried's astonished exclamation "Das ist kein Mann!" is astonishing, not comic. Disregarding Wagner, Rochaix has Siegfried flee his awakened bride; when Brünnhilde sings "Wer ist der Held, der mich erweckt? [Who is the hero who has awakened me?]," he stands, terrified, well outside her field of vision. Brünnhilde's gradual transformation from goddess to woman, Siegfried's coming to terms with adult feelings, their growing proximity, mutual awareness, and commitment—Rochaix's detailed understanding of all this, his use of blocking and gestural detail to bind the momentous, compressed emotional scenario, is a triumph of creative empathy.

Many at Seattle found Siegfried's interpolated pantomime/vision intrusive. The problem is partly Wagner's; his layoff partway through act 2 of *Siegfried* created discontinuities in the *Ring.* In particular, Siegfried and Brünnhilde became somewhat different personalities. Rochaix's masque intelligently attempts to explain the "new" Siegfried, whom Brünnhilde eventually praises for his loyalty and valor.

About another Rochaix insertion I have no reservations whatsoever. At the opening of Seattle's *Walküre,* the first person to walk onstage is Wotan, who does not figure in Wagner's version of act 1 (though an early sketch did include him). Entering through a door, he sits in a chair to the front and side of the stage and proceeds to watch Siegmund, Sieglinde, and Hunding enact their parts. The outcome startlingly illustrates Rochaix's ability to instill a fresh thinking-and-feeling response to familiar material. On the level of thinking, Wotan's tense scrutiny of events he has set in motion spotlights the *Ring*'s ongoing debate about free will versus predestination. On the level of feeling, seeing Siegmund through Wotan's eyes grafts a framework of poignant fatherly travail onto the feat-of-strength fairy tale of freeing a sword where others have failed. I found myself glancing at Wotan throughout Siegmund's tormented narrative; when the son describes the traumatic disappearance of his father and sole companion "Wolfe," it is precisely Wotan's quandary—the price of his power lust—that he cannot reveal himself and soothe the pain. I have never been so moved by Siegmund's despair as in Seattle.

Wotan's unsuspected impact is heightened, moreover, by a series of gestures precisely embodying his pride, anxiety, and control mania. For something like half an hour he sits erect and immobile, tensely vigilant, spear in hand. When, following Hunding's exit, Siegmund is stirred by memories that his father had pledged a rescuing sword, Wotan bends forward in his chair. Siegmund cries out: "Wälse! Wälse! Wo ist dein Schwert? [Where is your sword?]." Wotan lowers his spear toward Hunding's tree. A sudden flash of light illuminates Nothung. "Was gleisst dort hell im Glimmerschein? [What is that brightly gleaming in the flickering light?]," Siegmund exclaims, ecstatic. Wotan turns, stands, and exits. The door closes slowly behind him.

Wotan returns to his watching post to observe Siegfried during *Siegfried,* act 1. And in *Götterdämmerung,* act 1, Alberich occupies the same side stage. Standing legs apart, arms crossed, stealthy, frightened, brazen in Wotan's place, he is both dangerous and pathetic. His protégé Hagen, whom he observes, makes a sickening parallel to Wotan's Siegmund.

Another plus in Seattle's *Walküre,* act 1, is Rochaix's resourceful handling of Hunding's meal: his table manners, and also Siegmund's, are informative.

In his Bayreuth *Walküre,* Chéreau carried this idea further, making Hunding's eating behavior the central action in a characterization more incisive than Wagner's own. Hunding's attire—his fur-lined cape and vested suit—is itself suggestive; in conjunction with his coarse demeanor, it defines a parvenu. Stern, suspicious, sarcastic, he surrounds himself with threatening flunkies. Demanding Siegmund's name, he perches atop a long table and crosses his arms. Observing Sieglinde's eager interest in Siegmund—"sieh, wie gierig sie dich frägt! [Look how greedily she questions you!]"—he stabs an accusing finger at his wife; crouching, they eye one another like animals (so *this* is what Sieglinde means by an "ill-fated home"). During Siegmund's narrative, Hunding importantly shovels down his dinner, then casually picks his teeth with his fingers. But his nonchalance is feigned: he is at all times warily attentive, and so is his retinue, and so are we. His interjection—"Wunder und wilde Märe kündest du, kühner Gast, Wehwalt, der Wölfing! Mich dünkt, von dem wehrlichen Paar vernahm ich dunkle Sage, kannt' ich auch Wolfe und Wölfing nicht"—is a self-revealing outburst: The "mich dünkt [I imagine]" is knowing and aggressive, not conjectural. He slams the table, jangling the silverware. He drums his fingers on the tablecloth. He rises and paces rapidly. Fear takes hold: he retreats to the security of his flunkies, whose nervous arousal mirrors his own. Challenging Siegmund to combat, he overturns the table and shoves Sieglinde from the room. His exit line—"Hüte dich wohl! [Be on guard!]"— is delivered softly, tauntingly, with dilated nostrils. Chéreau clinches the characterization in act 2: after Wotan has speared Siegmund, Hunding circles the writhing, expiring body, then plants himself beside it and methodically stabs again and again. Like all the violence in Chéreau's *Ring,* Siegmund's murder is shockingly palpable; at Bayreuth the audience groaned and protested.

If updating or second-guessing Euripides, Shakespeare, and Ibsen seems less controversial than revisionist stagings of *Fidelio, Aïda,* and *Parsifal,* the reason is music: operas fix mood and cadence more than plays do. At worst, revisionist operatic directors turn a deaf ear to melody, harmony, timbre, rhythm—an evasion epitomized by Jean-Pierre Ponnelle's Halloween party version of *The Flying Dutchman,* seen at the Met in 1979. Though Rochaix and Chéreau are much better listeners, altering Wagner's action and stage pictures without altering his musical descriptions remains problematic.

For the transformation to scene 2 of *Rheingold,* Wagner asks that waves become clouds, then mist; I find Seattle's billowing, ascendant blue-taffeta curtain a feasible simplification. Seattle's spare, spacious scene 2—no "deep valley," "rocky summits," or "gleaming battlements"—suits the spare, spacious I–IV–V Valhalla cadence. For scene 3, Israel has designed a somber and mysterious Alberich house with the Tarnhelm music in mind. Rochaix closes the opera with a tableau—the gods ascend a ladder; Mime clambers out of a trap door; in the distance, Alberich eyes Fafner, who slowly packs his gold—sensitive to the B-flat minor vicissitudes shadowing Wagner's D-flat major close.* The high-spirited kitsch of Seattle's Ride of the Valkyries is a particular success; I cannot imagine a more unified seeing-and-hearing of this frivolous/ponderous music. For Waltraute's urgent reappearance in *Götterdämmerung,* however, her airborne carousel horse—contradicting Wagner, she does not dismount—superimposes unhelpful circus imagery. A bigger disappointment is Wotan's Farewell, seamless music set amid the discontinuous "backstage" clutter of Wotan's accessories and props. The culminating fire and smoke disregard the choreography of Wagner's Magic Fire, which audibly flashes, flickers, and glows. In fact, following the inspired "offstage" Wotan of *Walküre,* act 1, Rochaix's play-within-a-play conceit grows overdrawn and unsightly.

*In his *Richard Wagner's Music Dramas,* trans. Mary Whittal (Cambridge University Press, 1979), Dahlhaus memorably summarizes the ambiguity of this superficially triumphant ending: "Was [Wagner] looking through Loge's baleful eyes, or was he dazzled like the gods? The Rainbow Bridge motive consists of nothing more than a broken chord of G-flat major, extended over an entire period: a flickering but stationary sound, whose movement is all within itself. But whereas at the beginning of the work, in the E-flat major of the prelude, the simplicity was an allegory of the elemental universe and an image in sound of the primeval origin of things, at the end, after the music has been through so much development and elaboration, it creates the impression of reduction and of a simplification which is not to be trusted. It does not express certainty and firmness so much as self-deception about the disaster and confusion that lie behind the current state of affairs and will not be made to disappear by being ignored. The stationary sound that represents nature at the beginning is, at the end, 'second' nature, intended to draw a consoling veil over the story and its entanglements, but subject to the listener's reservations."

Chéreau, too, reinterprets Wagner's purely musical imagery with mixed results. His more radical deconstruction of Wagner's scenario dictates more radical violations of Romantic musical-dramatic unity. When in Chéreau's *Siegfried,* act 1, Siegfried's impotence—as I've noted, Wotan's machinery hammers Nothung for him—refutes his stentorian "Schmiede, mein Hammer, ein hartes Schwert! [Forge, my hammer, a hard sword!]," Chéreau savors the contradiction; poking fun at Siegfried and Wagner both, he turns the Forging Song into ironic drivel. Embedded in the mother-son parody played out by Mime and Siegfried, Chéreau's Siegfried parody is funny. But in *Götterdämmerung,* which contains no comedy, such episodes as Siegfried's Funeral Music and the Immolation scene prove unsalvageable: with Siegfried an irredeemable cipher, Wagner's heroic threnody becomes a non sequitur, and so does Brünnhilde's love death, with its salute to the dead hero. In the former case, Chéreau, ignoring the orchestra's march tread, makes do with having the Gibichungs stare at Siegfried's corpse and hoping that—as at the close of Friedrich's *Tannhäuser*—we are stirred to useful cogitation. Similarly, oblivious to Wagner's closure music, he ends *Götterdämmerung* with the Gibichungs lined up in front of the stage, staring the audience into some kind of response.

It's true enough that Wagner himself plagued *Götterdämmerung* with loose ends. Psychologically and dramatically, it is his weakest post-*Lohengrin* opera. It craves a "swimming" rendition, awash with unmediated waves of sheer feeling; Wagner himself, in a well-known letter, advised his friend August Röckel not to think too hard about Brünnhilde's final speech. Lacking believable heroes, or a believably human villain, *Götterdämmerung,* more than the other *Ring* operas, demands heroic singers. If Rochaix and Chéreau expose its weaknesses, its weaknesses expose their stubborn, counterproductive insistence on dramatic veracity. Wagner's letter to Röckel might have been addressed to Rochaix and Chéreau:

I do not agree with your criticisms with regard to a certain want of lucidity and distinctness of statement: on the contrary, I believe that a true instinct has kept me from a too-great definiteness; for it has been borne in on me that an absolute disclosing of the intention disturbs true insight. . . . You must feel that something is being enacted that is not to be expressed in mere words—and it is wrong of you to challenge me to explain it in words.*

The most obvious strength of the Rochaix and Chéreau *Ring*s is incisive characterization: the singers realize the force and complexity of their roles. The most blatant flaws arise from sweeping reconceptualizations of what happens and what it means. Couldn't a less reckless director separate the wheat from the chaff, retain the compelling foreground detail and throw out the revisionist backdrop? Maybe, but I doubt it.

In Ponnelle's *Flying Dutchman,* the revisionist backdrop is an ego trip, a new perspective for the hell of it: turn the opera into the Steersman's Dream and see what happens. What happens is that the Dutchman and Senta become distanced, imaginative figments unworthy of serious attention.† The experimentalism of

---

*And yet Wagner was not done reworking the already revised funeral speech.

†In the Bayreuth *Flying Dutchman* of Harry Kupfer—like Friedrich, a Felsenstein disciple—it is *Senta* who fantasizes the action of the opera. Unlike Ponnelle's dreaming Steersman, however, Kupfer's hallucinating Senta anchors an incisive reinterpretation: a case study in schizophrenia, replacing Wagner's Romantic legend prescribing redemption through love. Theatrically, the main beneficiaries of Kupfer's diagnosis are not the Dutchman and Senta, both powerfully realized by the composer, but the blandly sketched secondary characters. Realistically portrayed as unwitting perpetrators of Senta's derangement, Daland and the sailors' wives take on added significance. And the part of Erik is strengthened beyond recognition. Rather than a dull-witted plea, his pathetic cavatina is an act of compassion: "Don't you remember the day we met in the valley, and saw your father leave the shore?" he sings, desperate to yank Senta back to reality. But the narrow expectations of Erik and her father are the problem, not the cure; in panic, she visualizes the Dutchman as a defense. The subsequent trio, tugging equally in

Rochaix and Chéreau achieves an air of necessity: their alterations strive to explain and activate the drama. Rather than accepting Wagner at face value, they insist on immediacy, honesty, and nuanced theatricality. Even where their failures prove frustrating, we never feel harangued, used, or bored.

If Wotan is more craven than usual, it is because Rochaix and Chéreau take him seriously: they pay close attention to his rantings and come to their own conclusions. Especially in Chéreau's *Ring,* the same impulse for veracity, overthrowing convention and cliché, functions in microcosm at every turn. When Siegmund strains to dislodge Nothung, he really seems to be having trouble getting it out of the tree.

Chéreau's and Rochaix's updatings are embedded in this quest for detail and authenticity. In *Das Rheingold,* Rochaix's giants enter in a crate, lowered as if by an offstage crane. Their scruffy beards and workmen's clothes and tools contrast with the gods' natty or foppish attire. We recognize and know them before they have sung a word. Chéreau's Hunding tells us about himself by the way he uses a knife and fork. In two instances, Chéreau's humanized, modernized reportrayals open unsuspected avenues of empathy. Mime is a quick-tempered little Jew with wire-rimmed glasses and disheveled hair. He is fussy and devious, but never grotesque. His brief narrative of Siegfried's birth and Sieglinde's death ends with an unforgettable palms-up shrug on the words "Sie starb [She died]." His civilized irony makes him almost lik-

---

three directions, gains fresh power. The subtlest advantage of Kupfer's concept, especially beside Ponnelle's deafness, is its capacity to "explain" stylistic disparities in the score. The riper, more chromatic stretches are associated with the vigorously depicted fantasy world of Senta's mind; the squarer, more diatonic parts are framed by the dull walls of Daland's house, which collapse outward whenever Senta loses touch with reality. In the big Senta-Dutchman duet, where Wagner's stylistic lapses are particularly obvious, Kupfer achieves the same effect by alternating between Senta's fantasy of the Dutchman and the stolid, real-life suitor her father provides. It sounds fussy, but it works.

able. Alberich* is a grimy, potbellied opportunist in a floppy coat, too weak-headed to keep the ring (the ease with which Loge tricks him is, for once, completely believable), but abused and angry enough to curse it effectively. In *Götterdämmerung,* act 2, he does not challenge Hagen, but bows sheepishly before inquiring, "Schläfst du [Are you sleeping?], Hagen, mein Sohn?" On departing, rather than hissing demands, he pleads, "Sei treu! [Be true!]," with the anguish of one who knows the game is up, then shuffles slowly and confusedly offstage. Dominated by his futile greed and false hopes, Alberich is a poignant victim of the industrial age; he actually acquires tragic stature.

Upon reencountering the Met's *Tannhäuser* after seeing Friedrich's Bayreuth production in 1978, I was amazed by its generalized acting and blocking. The overall interpretation was more specifically Romantic-cathartic, to be sure, but what I mainly noticed was that, theatrically, it was less painstaking, less polished; it looked like an "opera," not a "play." Encountering the Met's new *Walküre* after seeing Seattle's *Ring,* I mainly noticed that the production made many fewer demands on the singers as actors.

Actually, the Schenk/Schneider-Siemssen *Tannhäuser* worked better than the Schenk/Schneider-Siemssen *Walküre.* Like *The Flying Dutchman* or *Lohengrin, Tannhäuser* is a Romantic opera with a historical locale. The *Ring* is antioperatic, ahistorical, metaphysical. In 1966 Wieland Wagner argued that "a naturalistic set today would simply destroy an illusion, not create one." It was likely, beforehand, that a "realistic" *Walküre* would fumble the *Winterstürme,* the Ride of the Valkyries, the costuming of the gods and goddesses. In the Met staging, the big door to Hunding's house "flies" open slowly, mechanically; the "spring night" it reveals has never seemed so hokey. For the Ride of the Valkyries, Schenk asks

*I am thinking of the late Zoltan Kelemen's 1978 performances. His replacement, Hermann Becht—the Chéreau Alberich documented on video and CD—is a less gripping artist.

for a lot of prancing and pointing at the (horseless) sky; Wagner's superbly descriptive music is wasted. Unsurprisingly, Rolf Langenfass, the costume designer, couldn't talk himself into winged and horned helmets: His uncertain headgear, robes, and skirts contradict Schneider-Siemssen's sets. In act 2 the busy, "realistic" clouds, which change color and shape with frantic speed, are a distraction. And I found the Magic Fire distinctly less musical than the more stylized Magic Fire in Schneider-Siemssen's previous *Walküre* at the Met: the 1967 production imported from Salzburg for Herbert von Karajan.

As for "Wagner's original intentions," in 1852–53 he wrote an essay detailing gestures and facial expressions for the Dutchman's monologue "Die Frist ist um." He begins:

> During the deep trumpet notes (B minor) at the close of the introductory scene [the Dutchman] has come offboard, along a plank lowered by one of the crew, to a shelf of rock on the shore; his rolling gait, proper to seafolk on first treading dry land after a long voyage, is accompanied by a wavelike figure. . . . With the first quarter note of the third bar he makes his second step—always with folded arms and sunken head; his third and fourth steps coincide with the notes of the eighth and tenth bars. From here on, his movements will follow the dictates of his general delivery, yet the actor must never let himself be betrayed into exaggerated striding to and fro: a certain terrible repose in outward demeanor, even amid the most passionate expression of inward anguish and despair, will give the characteristic stamp to this impersonation. The first phrases are to be sung without a trace of passion (almost in strict time, like the whole of this recitative), as though the man were tired out.

Wagner's score, however, is silent on these matters; the point of his essay is to show what type of creative intervention he expects from singers and directors. At the Met's *Walküre,* Schenk's direction seemed confined by Wagner's minimal staging and acting instructions. Following Wagner, Schenk's Siegmund occasionally rushes for the door, betraying impetuous vacillation. But he doesn't specifically evoke a starving, uncultivated outcast, as Rochaix's Siegmund does when he gobbles his food; or a self-conscious, sexually charged adolescent, as Chéreau's Siegmund does when he jumps up and away from Sieglinde's touch as she asks to see his wounds.

Andrew Porter, in a stimulating *New Yorker* review, suggested that the Met's stillborn *Walküre* may be a "neutral" staging waiting to be vitalized by singers "with the majesty and significance" of a Flagstad, Konetzni, or Hotter. I wonder. Peter Hofmann was a subtler, more ardent, more interesting Siegmund for Chéreau in Bayreuth than he is for Schenk in New York. Eva Marton's Bayreuth Elisabeth, under Friedrich, transcended the coarseness of her New York Elisabeth. Heinz Zednik, Chéreau's incomparable Mime, was a stereotypical evil dwarf in the 1981 Met *Siegfried.* Hildegard Behrens's efforts to make something honest and original out of Brünnhilde merely added a jarring note to the Met's *Walküre.* I don't doubt that something on the order of Jon Vickers's Siegmund could vitalize the production—but not more, and probably less, than Vickers might vitalize a *really* "neutral" presentation: in concert.

Previewing his production for *Opera News* in 1986, Schenk called *Die Walküre* "an immense love story, and the tragedy of a mighty father who must act against his heart." He decried the proliferation of European *Ring*s infected by "interpretitis." According to *Opera News*'s Gary Schmidgall, Schenk's *Walküre* would "banish the stiff, angular 'acting' that was common in the stark, symbol-laden productions of the 1950s and 1960s." Levine characterized the Met's previous, Salzburg-Karajan *Ring* as full of "symbolism nobody can explain," continuing: "We don't want to be reactionary and dull, we don't want to be negative and faddy." Bruce

Crawford, the Met's general manager, added: "We want what Wagner might have done if he had been blessed with our facilities."

To dismiss, as "interpretitis," the post-Wieland revisionism of Rochaix, Chéreau, Friedrich, or Kupfer wastes valuable opportunities for engagement. "Stiff, angular 'acting'" was long ago "banished" from *Ring* stagings everywhere but at the Met, which retained its quasi–New Bayreuth *Walküre* through 1983—a production free of "symbolism," inexplicable or otherwise. As for "what Wagner might have done"—any twentieth-century reconsideration of Wagner's intentions must account for what Dahlhaus, in *The New Grove Wagner,* rightly calls his "aesthetic demand for innovation." "The postulate of originality," Dahlhaus continues, "the dominant aesthetic belief of the day, meant not only that music should proceed out of the composer's own emotions, but also that it should be novel in order to rank as authentic."

The Met's resistance to contemporary culture creates a false impression of opera as intellectually undernourished, necessarily digressive from life. The merest glance at opera's institutional history shows this isn't so. The vitality of Gustav Mahler's Vienna Opera (1897–1907) was assured not merely through its matter-of-course sponsorship of new works. Like Mahler himself, Alfred Roller, his principal designer, was a member in good standing of Vienna's high-cultural vanguard; his art nouveau costumes and stylized sets overthrew canons of verisimilitude. Otto Klemperer's Kroll Opera (1927–33) resonated with the prevailing *Neue Sachlichkeit.* When Jenkins mounted *Salome* in Seattle in 1986, he chose Seattle's Mark Morris to choreograph the Dance of the Seven Veils. At the Brooklyn Academy of Music, host to New York's Next Wave Festival, Morris may be the most highly regarded American choreographer of his generation. Morris and other Next Wave artists debunk the solemnity of traditional high culture. They reject the self as subject, the Romantic cult of individualism. They hold every text equivocal, finding unintended meanings, distrusting obvious or single interpretations. Even as directors of *Der Ring des Nibelungen,* Rochaix and Chéreau would be more at home in New York at BAM than at the Metropolitan Opera.

If it seems too much to ask the Met to be postmodern, must *all* the company's Wagner productions be, in Mann's phrase, "politically innocent" of Wagner's "roots-in-the-soil," "mythical-reactionary revolutionism"? Even if it must reject "interpretitis," has the Met considered such lesser Seattle heresies as concealing the orchestra under an opaque scrim, banishing white shirts from the pit, eliminating all but last-act curtain calls? And then there are Seattle's supertitles. Setting aside the controversy over supertitles versus opera in English: never, before Seattle, had I encountered so focused an American Wagner audience. Throughout Wotan's exchange with Fricka, during Wotan's monologue, the house was rapt, hanging on every word. Such a listening environment stimulates everyone, including the singing actors. Jenkins told me Rochaix directed the Seattle *Ring* "with the supertitles in mind."

The rationale for the Metropolitan Opera, opened in 1883, was social, not artistic: a new stratum of New York wealth wanted prestige-bearing opera boxes, and the opera boxes at the Academy of Music were full. An early policy of opera in German was dictated by expedience. Afterward came a polyglot status quo. French houses did Verdi in French; German houses did Gounod in German; Italian houses did Wagner in Italian. But the Met did not perform Verdi, Gounod, or Wagner in English. Early Met audiences, significantly, included droves of first-generation Germans and Italians. If later Met audiences found the singers' German and Italian increasingly incomprehensible, it hardly mattered: the Met bathed in a sea of vocal opulence. Treated as showcases for Melchior and Flagstad, Ponselle and Martinelli, the operas of Wagner and Verdi were more cloaked than revealed by their inviolable, indecipherable words. At the same time, this magically remote verbal patina was by no means useless. Even after 1937, when the Metropolitan Opera Auditions of the Air began propelling dozens of American singers into the company's ranks, the Met mainly continued to reject sung English. Granted, there were artistic and practical reasons for singing the words the composer himself set, but these were not the only reasons; opera seemed more certifiably genuine in foreign tongues.

The very size of the 3,615-seat auditorium, dwarfing the famous opera houses of Europe, catered to heroic vocalism while discouraging the verbal nuance and gestural subtlety of theater. When the Met moved to Lincoln Center in 1966, its new home enlarged the old Met's gargantuan dimensions by 125 seats and brightened the interior with a Cadillac glamour recalling its nouveau riche beginnings. Yet Goeran Gentele, named to become general manager following Rudolf Bing's departure in 1972, offered great hopes for change. At Stockholm's Royal Opera, Gentele's successes as general manager had included an ingenious *Ballo in maschera* in which Gustav III was (as in history) a homosexual; a *Rake's Progress* staged by Ingmar Bergman and admired by Stravinsky; and the premiere of Karl-Birger Blomdahl's space-age *Aniara,* staged, like the revisionist *Ballo,* by Gentele himself. Gentele wanted to modernize the Met's repertoire. He planned a much-needed 280-seat "Piccolo Met." He hired a major conductor—Rafael Kubelik—to be the first supervising music director since Toscanini. He engaged Leonard Bernstein to conduct his premiere production, an innovative *Carmen* centered on Don José and restoring the spoken dialogue. But Gentele was killed in an automobile accident in 1972, and Kubelik quit two years later.

James Levine, appointed "principal conductor" by Gentele, wound up the thirty-three-year-old music director in 1976. He went to work with limitless enthusiasm. He dramatically improved the orchestra and chorus. He saw that Berg, Debussy, Poulenc, and Weill were performed. In the pit, he achieved especially satisfying results in massive, majestic scores like *Don Carlos* and *Parsifal.* Compared to what was going on at the New York Philharmonic and New York City Opera, the Met was seen fighting the good fight; its failures received the benefit of the doubt.

Ten years after Levine's appointment, however, the nipped-in-the-bud Gentele regime more than ever seems a lost opportunity to have treated opera as theater, to have introduced contemporary repertoire, to have engaged world-class conductors, to have tested, gambled, and grappled as with a living art form. The lingering prejudice against "interpretitis" is symptomatic of a lingering provincialism that Gentele might have expunged, and that is now expunged in America's "provinces." When Seattle began its Wagner festival in 1975, the first *Ring* production, conducted by Henry Holt, brandished a "traditionalism" contradicting Bayreuth's revisionism: a typical New World move, reflecting insecure, hands-off appropriation of Old World art. In hiring Rochaix and Israel, Jenkins brought Seattle into line with hands-on European practice: not art as a "timeless" museum piece, symbolizing cultural achievement, but—taking cultural achievement for granted—art as a workable clay.

Meanwhile, the Met's aged, uninquisitive audience holds new productions hostage to the gratuitous opulence of a Franco Zeffirelli *Tosca* or *La Bohème,* or a Schenk/Schneider-Siemssen *Tales of Hoffmann.* "Wagner experienced modern culture, the culture of bourgeois society, through the medium and in the image of the operatic theater of his day," wrote Mann.

> He saw art reduced to the level of an extravagant consumer product . . . he watched with fury while vast resources were squandered, not for the attainment of high artistic purpose, but for that which he despised above all else as an artist: the easy, cheap effect. And because he saw that none of this offended anyone else as it offended him, he concluded that the political and social conditions that could bring forth such things, and to which they properly belonged, were utterly vile—and must be changed by revolutionary means.

Perhaps the means for changing the Met still exist; Peter Sellars, America's answer to Chéreau and Rochaix, is tentatively scheduled to direct Bartók's *Bluebeard's Castle,* Schoenberg's *Erwartung,* and Debussy's *Martyrdom of St. Sebastian* at the Met in 1988–89.* And yet: the more meaningfully subversive Sellars's stagings prove, the more will they be out of place. Like Rochaix's or Chéreau's Wagner, Sellars's triple bill more likely belongs at Brooklyn Academy of Music, or with one of America's regional companies, or at any number of European houses whose audiences are less accustomed to glamour and glitz, "swimming" and "sleepwalking."

(1987)

---

*Sellars withdrew from the project.

3 · *Dvořák and the New World*

A Concentrated Moment

Though little remembered today, even by musicians, Antonín Dvořák's New York was a world music capital. A century ago, the New York Philharmonic enjoyed unprecedented artistic and financial prosperity. The Metropolitan Opera had entered its "Golden Age." New York was inundated with phenomenal vocalists and instrumentalists. Its orchestras and opera houses eagerly presented important premieres. As never since, music was central to the city's intellectual life. Concert-giving and operagoing were, more than rites of habit, a necessary response to aesthetic urges and emotional needs.

Three individuals—Anton Seidl, Jeannette Thurber, and Henry Krehbiel—collectively suggest the reasons that New York stirred and seduced Dvořák.

Seidl, born in Budapest in 1850, was one of the leading conductors of the late nineteenth century. For a dozen years following his arrival in 1885, he was New York's most influential musician. At the Metropolitan Opera, he presided over six historic German-language seasons, during which the German ensemble arguably surpassed any in Europe. With the New York Philharmonic, at the Brooklyn Academy, at Coney Island's Brighton Beach resort, he was also New York's leading concert conductor. The most important musician ever to visit the United States and stay, he became an American citizen, bought a country house in the Catskills, and would not be addressed as "Herr." His "Americamania" included a fondness for mixed drinks and excited approbation of the prospective Spanish-American War. He befriended Edward MacDowell, and—in an excess of partisanship for the Wagner cause he extolled—called MacDowell greater than Brahms. He championed opera in English as a necessary step toward the production of important American operas. He called for an elaborate system of musical education to counteract the harmful influence of itinerant foreign artists. A suitable opera school, he wrote, "would keep at home those young musicians"—not only singers but also conductors and instrumentalists—"who annually go abroad to study." Seidl himself embarked on a Wagnerian music drama, to a libretto in English, based on the Hiawatha legend. His goal for the United States was a "national music," "an individual musical art."

If Seidl's opera school never materialized, its nearest equivalent was Jeannette Thurber's New York–based National Conservatory of Music, where Seidl taught conducting. Thurber was a visionary. No less than Seidl, she dreamed of rescuing American music from possessive European parents. Her wealthy husband, the food merchant Francis Beattie Thurber, sympathized. With his financial help, she had in 1885 established the American Opera Company—an opera-in-English venture designed to subvert the snob appeal of Old World divas and foreign tongues. Emphasizing American singers, affordable ticket prices, and integrated musical theater, the American Opera Company survived for two hectically administered yet artistically rewarding seasons (see pages 168–70). Much longer-lived was the National Conservatory, begun the same year. Having herself attended the Paris Conservatory, Thurber poured time and money into creating a thorough music school for Americans. In addition to Seidl, the faculty included the pianist Rafael Joseffy (himself a student of Moscheles and Tausig), the composers Horatio Parker (later dean of the School of Music at Yale) and Rubin Goldmark (later head of the composition department at Juilliard), and the influential critics James Gibbons Huneker (who taught piano) and Henry Finck (who taught music history).

Thurber's agenda stressed the self-sufficiency of an American musical education. She espoused an American idiom based on native sources. She offered scholarships for women, minorities, and the handicapped. African-American students were prominent at every level of study. Campaigning for a congressional charter, she gave a concert of works by Americans, including Dudley Buck and John Knowles Paine. Enactment of this unusual legislation, in 1891, was heralded as a landmark commitment to American art. Thurber's personal charm played no small role in winning these and other victories. "She was a picturesque woman," Huneker would recall. "She spoke French like a Parisian, and . . . I confess that her fine, dark eloquent eyes troubled my peace more than once."

New York's central arbiter of musical taste, and the acknowledged dean of American music critics, was Henry Krehbiel of the *Tribune*. He was one of Anton Seidl's few intimate friends. Like Seidl, with whom he conversed in German, he paid complex dual allegiance to the Old World of Beethoven and Wagner and a new world of American musical prospects. Like Seidl and Thurber (whose opera company he accurately faulted for poor management and for the "impudent exaggeration" of its "claims to excellence"), he advocated opera in English as one component of an integrated musical theater contradicting meretricious vocal glamour.

In common with Seidl and Thurber, Krehbiel embraced contemporary notions of cultural nationalism. He maintained that a nation's highest expression in art, music, and literature was to some degree a function of "race": "Like tragedy in its highest conception, music is of all times and all peoples; but the more the world comes to realize how deep and intimate are the springs from which the emotional element of music flows, the more fully will it recognize that originality and power in the composer rest upon the use of dialects and idioms which are national or racial in origin and structure." An autodidact of vast erudition, Krehbiel made himself a virtual ethnomusicologist. Documenting the relationship of folk song to national schools of composition, he researched and wrote about the folk music of Magyars, Slavs, Scandinavians, Russians, Orientals, and American Indians. Of special interest are his findings regarding "Afro-American folk songs," which he began publishing in the *Tribune* in 1899 and which in 1914 generated a 155-page book—not a vague armchair rumination but a closely argued report packed with scrutiny of modes, rhythms, and the like. Krehbiel hoped America's composers would appropriate plantation songs. He rebuked as "ungenerous and illiberal" those culture-bearers who balked at equating "negro" and "American."*

Enter Dvořák. Jeannette Thurber was the agent of his coming. The first director of the National Conservatory, the baritone Jacques Bouy (who created the role of Escamillo), had returned to Paris in 1889. Thurber needed an eminent replacement. Dvořák was not only eminent; with his rustic roots and egalitarian temperament, he was the kind of cultural nationalist to inspire Americans. She offered him fifteen thousand dollars for each of two years. When Dvořák declined she went into high gear, besieging him with letters and emissaries until he capitulated. Dvořák arrived in New York on September 27, 1892, the most prominent composer ever to take up a teaching post in the United States. He proved inquisitive and empathetic, as eager to learn as to teach. His aspirations for American music resonated with the hopes of

---

*Henry Krehbiel, "Antonín Dvořák," *Century Magazine,* September 1892, and *Afro-American Folksongs: A Study in Racial and National Music* (New York, 1911), p. vii. Krehbiel deplored ragtime, however, as a gross popularization that nevertheless proved "that a marvelous potency lies in the characteristic rhythmical element of the slave songs." He came to associate jazz with "negro brothels of the south" and affirmed that it encouraged instrumental techniques—"unnatural contortion of the lips and forcing of the breath"—unsuited to the higher purposes he wished African-American music to serve.

Thurber, Seidl, and Krehbiel. A concerted mandate was mutually pursued.

The climactic moment in Dvořák's American career came on December 16, 1893—the premiere of his *New World* Symphony at Carnegie Music Hall, with Seidl leading the New York Philharmonic. The concert was the most famous the Philharmonic gave during Seidl's tenure. The symphony—still the most famous composed on American soil—encapsulates Dvořák's agenda for America.

As early as September 1892—the month Dvořák arrived aboard the S.S. *Saale*—Krehbiel wrote in *Century Magazine:* "In Dvořák and his works is to be found a twofold encouragement for the group of native musicians whose accomplishments of late have seemed to herald the rise of a school of American composers. . . . There is measureless comfort in the prospect which the example of Dvořák has opened up." The following month, at Carnegie Music Hall, the National Conservatory honored Dvořák at a concert including Liszt's *Tasso,* conducted by Seidl, and Dvořák's *Te Deum,* conducted by Dvořák. Krehbiel wrote in the *Tribune* that Dvořák "found ready to greet him an assemblage that crowded the splendid concert room entered with fervor into the spirit of the unique occasion. . . . nearly all of the musicians of note in the city were present." Krehbiel's American pride, which frequently suffered outrage in the face of European neglect, also spurred him to observe that

> the eminent musician who has cast his lot temporarily with us had no cause to question the sincerity and heartiness of the welcome which was extended to him and less to be dissatisfied with the manner in which his music was performed. It is a question whether he has ever stood before an orchestra that was quicker in understanding his wishes, or more willing and able to fulfil them than the eighty men in the band last night, the great majority of

whom belonged to Mr. Seidl's metropolitan organization. In respect of ability to read and grasp the contents of new music, the orchestral players of New-York may truthfully be said to be without peers.

In fact, no less than Seidl before him, Dvořák swiftly absorbed what musical New York had to offer. In subsequent concerts, twice leading his Symphony in D minor, op. 70, he had occasion to test Seidl's conviction that New York's pool of superb orchestral musicians surpassed that of any European city. He also led his *Requiem* with Artur Nikisch's magnificent Boston Symphony. Meanwhile, the frequent visitors at his home on East Seventeenth Street included the twenty-five-year-old Harry Burleigh. Attracted by Jeannette Thurber's scholarships for African Americans, Burleigh had enrolled at the National Conservatory in mid-1892. Dvořák savored the spirituals and Stephen Foster songs Burleigh sang for him; his favorites included "Swing Low, Sweet Chariot," which he seemingly adapted in the E minor Symphony he was then composing in sympathy with Thurber's suggestion that he "write a symphony embodying his experiences and feelings in America." The principal subject of the slow movement—a tune so resembling a spiritual that it later, as "Goin' Home," became one—was entrusted to the English horn, whose reedy timbre, it has been suggested, resembled Burleigh's voice.

On May 21—three days before he completed the *New World* Symphony—Dvořák was extensively quoted in the *New York Herald* in "On the Real Value of Negro Melodies." "'I am now satisfied,' he said . . . 'that the future music of this country must be founded upon what are called the negro melodies. This must be the real foundation of any serious and original school of composition to be developed in the United States. When I first came here last year I was impressed with this idea and it has developed into a settled conviction.'" The same article cited Thurber's declaration that "the aptitude of the colored race for music, vocal and instrumental, has long been recognized, but no definite steps have hitherto been taken to develop it, and it is believed that the decision of the conservatory to move in this new direction will meet with general approval and be productive of prompt and encouraging results." On May 28, in a letter to the *Herald,* Dvořák added: "It is to the poor that I turn for musical greatness. The poor work hard; they study seriously. . . . If in my own career I have achieved a measure of success and reward it is to some extent due to the fact I was the son of poor parents and was reared in an atmosphere of struggle and endeavour." (Krehbiel later commented that Dvořák's life had been "a story of manifest destiny, of signal triumph over obstacle and discouraging environment," that Dvořák had triumphed "by an exercise of traits of mind and character that have always been peculiarly the admiration of American manhood.")

On June 3 Dvořák left New York for Spillville, Iowa, a Czech settlement where he encountered the touring Kickapoo Medicine Show, including chanting American Indians and two "niggers" who danced and sang with banjo and guitar. He returned to the National Conservatory the following September. In November, Seidl secured permission from Dvořák to give the first performance of the *New World* Symphony and scheduled the premiere. In preparing the piece, Seidl formed the opinion that the second movement expressed homesickness for Bohemia. His languid tempo may have been the reason Dvořák changed the marking from *larghetto* to *largo.*

Krehbiel hailed the new symphony in a 2,500-word article in the *Tribune* on December 15. At the time, Krehbiel and Dvořák were constantly in touch. Krehbiel spoke for them both when he wrote:

> That which is most characteristic, most beautiful and most vital in our folk-song has come from the negro slaves of the South, partly because those slaves lived in the period of emotional, intellectual and social development which produces folk-song, partly because they lived a life that

prompted utterance in song and partly because as a race the negroes are musical by nature. Being musical and living a life that has in it romantic elements of pleasure as well as suffering, they gave expression to those elements in songs which reflect their original nature as modified by their American environment.

In the ensuing exegesis, Krehbiel explored "negro" and "American" traits of the new work. He also remarked that "if there is anything Indian about Dr. Dvořák's symphony it is only in the mood inspired by the contemplation of Indian legend and romance, and that is outside the sphere of this discussion." By this he apparently meant that Dvořák relied on no vernacular specimens. An article in the *Herald* the same day cited Dvořák's own testimony that his second and third movements were influenced by Longfellow's *The Song of Hiawatha,* which he had first encountered, in translation, thirty years before. He also indicated that he envisioned composing a Hiawatha opera or cantata. (In fact, Thurber secured permission from Alice M. Longfellow for Dvořák to use the poem. But Dvořák progressed less far on his Hiawatha project than Seidl did on his; according to Huneker, Seidl managed to finish one act of music before his death.)*

A "public rehearsal" (actually, a first performance) of the *New*

---

*Musical Courier, April 6, 1898. Following a suggestion by Krehbiel, Seidl's opera started not with Longfellow's version of the Hiawatha story but with the Iroquois legend connecting Hiawatha with the founding of the Confederacy of the Five Nations. The result would be an operatic trilogy, an "American *Nibelungenlied.*" Seidl procured examples of Indian music from Krehbiel. His librettist was Francis Nielson, later the stage manager at Covent Garden. Curiously, in his article "Wagner's Influence on Present-Day Composers" (*North American Review,* January 1894), Seidl commented regarding the United States that "this country is so young that its history does not afford material for great conceptions as do the European countries, rich in legend and tradition. One might go for material back to the Indians, but it would be pretty thin; it would be lacking in those majestic elements which Wagner found in the Norse legends."

World Symphony took place on December 15. For the formal premiere the following evening, Dvořák was present. After the second movement, the packed house erupted in applause. Seidl turned to gesture toward Dvořák's box. "Every neck was craned so that it might be discovered to whom he was motioning so energetically," reported the *Herald.*

> Whoever it was, he seemed modestly to wish to remain at the back of the box on the second tier.
>
> At last a broad shouldered individual of medium height, and as straight as one of the pines in the forests of which his music whispered so eloquently, is descried by the eager watchers. A murmur sweeps through the hall. "Dvořák! Dvořák!" is the word that passes from mouth to mouth. . . .
>
> With hands trembling with emotion Dr. Dvořák waves an acknowledgement of his indebtedness to Anton Seidl, to the orchestra, to the audience, and then disappears into the background while the remainder of the work goes on. . . . At its close the composer was loudly called for. Again and again he bowed his acknowledgements, and again and again the applause burst forth.
>
> Even after he had left his box and was walking about in the corridor the applause continued. And finally he returned to the gallery railing, and then what a reception he received! The musicians, led by Mr. Seidl, applauded until the place rang again.

The critic—presumably Albert Steinberg, like Krehbiel a close friend of Seidl—called the work itself "a great one" and distinctively American in flavor. Krehbiel, in the *Tribune,* decreed it "a lovely triumph" and wrote of the new symphony's indebtedness to African-American song. A signature trait of both reviews— and of others in the daily press—was the detailed description of musical content. Of the *Herald* critic's twenty-six paragraphs, twelve analyzed Dvořák's idiom (the flatted seventh tone of his scale, etc.), his folk sources, rhythms and harmonies, instrumentation, and structure. To the performance of the new work, the *Herald* critic allotted a single sentence, terming it "most poetical." He dispatched the remainder of the program with a sentence reading: "The orchestra played the 'Midsummer Night's Dream' music, and Henri Marteau played Brahm's [*sic*] violin concerto with an original cadenza by himself." This eager concentration on new music documents a moment, a century ago, when composer and audience were one.

Dvořák's example focused a debate that had grown vigorous, sophisticated, and dense. The general intellectual discourse of newspapers and magazines already routinely scrutinized America's concert and opera life, stressing issues of taste and identity. Wagnerian progress toward unified musical theater, away from gaudy vocal display, was one frequent topic. Another concerned the proper sources of a native compositional idiom: should it be consciously nationalistic, or would some ineffable folk essence ultimately inflect American music without special effort? Rejecting Dvořák's advocacy of the first strategy, genteel critics such as Boston's William Foster Apthorp and genteel composers such as Boston's John Knowles Paine dismissed cultural nationalism as quasi-barbaric. In cosmopolitan New York, where American Indian and African-American influences seemed more picturesque, less exogenous, the response was more favorable.* Of America's composers,

---

*W. J. Henderson's three-thousand-word review of the *New World* Symphony, in the December 17, 1893, *New York Times*, remains one of the most vivid and sympathetic descriptions of the work ever written. It is also wonderfully free of racial bias, reading in part: "In spite of all assertions to the contrary, the plantation songs of the American negro possess a striking individuality. No matter whence their germs came, they have in their growth been subjected to local influences which have made of them a new species. That species is the direct result of causes climatic and political, but never anything else than American. Our South is ours. Its twin does not exist. Our system of slavery, with all its domestic and racial conditions, was ours, and its twin never existed. Out of the heart of this slavery,

the prominent Indianist Arthur Farwell considered himself "the first composer in America to take up Dvořák's challenge . . . in a serious and whole-hearted way." Farwell revered Seidl, who helped guide his musical education.

Dvořák returned to Bohemia in May for the summer. He resumed his duties in New York the following October, then left the United States for good in April 1895. In addition to the *New World* Symphony, his American output included his best-known string quartet, in F major, and his best-known concerto, for cello in B minor. The latter was partly inspired by the Second Cello Concerto of Victor Herbert. Dvořák heard the premiere, performed by the composer with Seidl conducting the New York Philharmonic, in March 1894. Herbert was Seidl's principal cellist and sometime assistant conductor. He eventually wrote an opera, *Natoma* (1911), on American Indian themes. As an important conductor of the Pittsburgh Orchestra and of his own Victor Herbert Orchestra, he was a Seidl protégé.

To what degree Dvořák's compositional style was influenced by his American stay is a good question. Though his kinship to Brahms is often contemplated, in New York Dvořák did not seem Brahmsian. Seidl, who dismissed Brahms much as Hugo Wolf did in Vienna, renewed Dvořák's interest in Wagner. With its programmatic complexion the *New World* Symphony represents a turning point toward the tone poems and operas Dvořák later

---

environed by this sweet and languorous South, from the canebrake and the cotton field, arose the spontaneous musical utterance of a people. That folk-music struck an answering note in the American heart. The most popular of all American composers was he who came nearest to a reproduction of it—Stephen Foster. The American people—or the majority of them—learned to love the songs of the negro slave and to find in them something that belonged to America. If those songs are not national, then there is no such thing as national music. . . . Dr. Dvořák has penetrated the spirit of this music, and with themes suitable for symphonic treatment, he has written a beautiful symphony, which throbs with American feeling."

composed. Like the *American* String Quartet, this last Dvořák symphony eschews the denser motivic and contrapuntal interplay of earlier, more Brahmsian works. It was in America, too, that Dvořák, assisted by the Wagnerite critic Henry Finck, authored an essay on Schubert whose seven references to Wagner compare to only three to Brahms.

An especially vivid example of Dvořák's American style is the third movement of the little-known *American* Suite for solo piano, composed in New York in 1894. Here is music dramatically different from any Dvořák could have created in Europe. As in his well-known G-flat *Humoresque* (conceived in Iowa but set down in Bohemia in 1895), a skipping tune evokes a happy-go-lucky "plantation dance"—such as one of those already composed by his African-American student Maurice Arnold. The striding left hand is a second popular American signature (Dvořák almost certainly heard ragtime in New York and Chicago). The subsidiary lyric material, with its pentatonic flavor and occasional "Scotch snap" (that is, a stressed short note on the beat followed by a longer note), is in Dvořák's "Indian" mode. These localized thematic and rhythmic features are only half the story. The pentatonic scale and Scotch snap permeate the music Dvořák composed in New York and Spillville—and also (if less markedly) in Prague. But the texture of the American works is new. The plain attire and often startling simplicity of Dvořák's American style partly suggest pedagogical intent. Krehbiel, in the January 13, 1894, *New York Tribune,* commented that the *American* Quartet and E-flat Quintet (both composed in 1893) were "compacter and simpler in form" than the earlier A major Sextet (1878), more "direct," less "labored," so that "the composers, who may undertake to work on the lines which [Dvořák] has marked out, may have the clearest model before them." (A year later, Dvořák himself wrote that in his *American* Quartet he "wanted for once to write something very melodious and simple.") More provocative, more profound, is the influence of the American landscape, of which Dvořák wrote from Spillville:

It is very strange here . . . especially in the prairies there are only endless acres of field and meadow. That's all you see. . . . you don't meet a soul, and you're glad to see the huge herds of cattle in the woods and meadows which in summer and winter are out to pasture in the broad fields. And so, it is very wild here, and sometimes very sad, sad to despair.

Never before had Dvořák encountered such a vast unpopulated terrain. Its openness and vacancy—what Henderson, reviewing the *New World* Symphony, experienced as "the melancholy of our Western wastes"; what Willa Cather, describing the effect of the *New World* Symphony in her novel *The Song of the Lark* (1915), called "the immeasurable yearning of all flat lands"—are embodied in the clean sonority and uncluttered, unadorned musical space of Dvořák's American style.

Dvořák's final thoughts about "Music in America" were published in *Harper's* in February 1895. He praised musical Americans for their aptitude and enthusiasm but lamented the absence of governmental support for musical instruction and performance. He castigated the Metropolitan Opera as a company that "only the upper classes can hear or understand" and called for "opera companies where native singers can be heard, and where the English tongue is sung." Seidl, Krehbiel, and Thurber equally understood that, otherwise, no important American operas would be written. No less than Dvořák, who avoided the Met as a rich man's preserve, Seidl, Krehbiel, and Thurber impugned operatic tinsel and glamour. Krehbiel complained of the "domination of fashion instead of love for art," Seidl of "the rich who [regard] music as a mere diversion." Both Seidl and Krehbiel profoundly comprehended, with Dvořák, that reliance on vast individual wealth ultimately acted to discourage an indigenous musical high culture.

That this mattered to Dvořák—that, like Seidl, he was no mere interloper—was a crucial source of American gratitude and affection. Far more typical was the case of the next major European composer to take an American position: Gustav Mahler, who during his years with the Met and the New York Philharmonic (1907–11) summered at home in Europe, and for whom the composition of a *New World* Symphony would have been unthinkable. In decades to come, an army of important Europeans followed, ranging in attitude from Ernst Křenek, who held American culture in something like contempt, to Kurt Weill, who refused to speak German from the day he arrived. Most of the prominent immigrant composers were modernists for whom cultural nationalism—and, concomitantly, the search for an American idiom—was passé. Few and far between were such New World portraits as Ernest Bloch's *America: An Epic Rhapsody* (1928), Paul Hindemith's *Pittsburgh* Symphony (1958), and Darius Milhaud's *A Frenchman in New York* (1962). Even had they been more musically distinguished, these contributions could not possibly have made such a formidable impact as had Dvořák's famous symphony. After World War I, classical music in the United States was increasingly marginalized by popular culture. At the same time, a democratized new audience for classical music preferred canonized European masters to contemporary or American creators. The quest for a distinctly American musical high culture would never again be the consolidated priority it seemed to Dvořák, Seidl, Krehbiel, and Thurber and to their readers, listeners, and students.

Seidl did not long survive Dvořák's leave-taking from America; he died in 1898 at the age of forty-seven. His final season with the New York Philharmonic included performances of the *New World* Symphony. He had earlier repeated the work with the Philharmonic in 1894 and had introduced it to Brooklyn to great acclaim. Krehbiel once wrote to Dvořák that he had "had no greater happiness from 20 years of labor on behalf of good music than has come to me from the consciousness that I may have been to some degree instrumental in helping the public to appreciate your compositions, and especially the [*New World*] Symphony." Following Seidl's death and the onset of twentieth-century fragmentation, Krehbiel gradually lost enthusiasm for New York's world of music; he died dispirited in 1923. Thurber wrote in 1919 that "in looking back over my 35 years of activity as President of the National Conservatory of Music of America there is nothing I am so proud of as having been able to bring Dr. Dvořák to America." Her school never regained the dominant role it enjoyed during Dvořák's directorship. It was declared officially defunct in 1952, six years after Thurber's death at the age of ninety-five.

After World War I the world of American music of which Dvořák, Seidl, Thurber, and Krehbiel were part was forgotten. A new generation of American composers gravitated toward Paris and Nadia Boulanger, modernism and jazz. Germanic models—Brahms, Wagner, Dvořák—were spurned, and so were their New World offshoots Paine, Chadwick, MacDowell, and Beach. Memory of Dvořák's visit was all but erased, and his Symphony *From the New World* was returned to Europe. Countless commentaries (I remember them from record jackets) insisted it was typically Czech, a Dvořák symphony like any other.

Leonard Bernstein, in one 1960s essay, parodistically dissected the *New World* Symphony's ostensible "American" traits and discovered not Indians and negroes, but *Tannhäuser,* Brahms's First, Mussorgsky's *Pictures at an Exhibition,* and Schubertian beer hall music. The *New World* Symphony, he concluded, is French, German, Russian, Chinese, Scottish—anything you please. Bernstein was correct to stress that Dvořák's native language was European. But he turned a deaf ear to Dvořák's American accent.

As recently as 1990 the latest critical edition of the *New World* Symphony, published by Breitkopf & Härtel, insisted that the symphony's most typical features "turn out to be just as typical of Czech music." A year later, Dvořák's East Seventeenth Street residence was demolished when the New York City Council overrode a recommendation by the city's Landmarks Preservation Commission. This cultural vandalism was supported by a *New York Times* editorial titled "Dvořák Doesn't Live Here Anymore."

It took the centennial of Dvořák's New World visit to counteract seventy-five years of amnesia. Dvořák's contribution to America was celebrated at festivals in Spillville, in Iowa City, at Bard College, at Lincoln Center, and at the Brooklyn Academy of Music. Two essay collections—*Dvořák in America* (1993), edited by John Tibbetts, and *Dvořák and His World* (1993), edited by Michael Beckerman—valuably renew impressions of Dvořák in New York and Spillville, as does Robert Winter's ingenious computerized "companion" to the *New World* Symphony, published in 1994. It seems there may even be a Hollywood film, in which Dvořák's unrequited love for his sister-in-law—perhaps apocryphal, perhaps not—is a major thematic thread. As it becomes known, a single piece of recent Dvořák scholarship will change forever the way we hear the *New World* Symphony's scherzo. Extrapolating from Dvořák's testimony that the symphony's middle movements were based on scenes from the *Song of Hiawatha,* Michael Beckerman has shown that the scherzo's whirling-and-hopping trajectory and skittish dance tune, with a "primitive" five-note compass; its incessant tom-tom and exotic drone; and the accelerating energy of its initial crescendo programmatically represent the Beggar's Dance of "Hiawatha's Wedding Feast":

Treading softly like a panther.
Then more swiftly and still swifter,
Whirling, spinning round in circles
Leaping o'er the guests assembled,
Eddying round and round the wigwam,

> Till the leaves went whirling with him,
> Till the dust and wind together
> Swept in eddies round about him.

The Dvořák centenary, finally, supports a larger reclamation project: the rediscovery of turn-of-the-century America, when music was "queen of the arts," and Union Square was a teeming community of culture; when a world-class Wagner movement, presided over by Seidl, galvanized a mixed audience of genteel intellectuals and New American Women; when the Metropolitan Opera entered its "Golden Age"; when Chadwick and Beach wrote symphonies more stirring and authentic than many composed by more famous American symphonists of the 1930s and 1940s; when Charles Ives, a singular offshoot of genteel schooling, wrote his first important music.

This American fin de siècle failed to impress subsequent generations of Americans because—unlike the fin de siècle movements of Europe—it resisted modernism. Its emphasis on the morality of art has been held up to ridicule by legions of twentieth-century artists and intellectuals. And yet today the saga of Dvořák in America appeals partly because of the high moral purpose that he exuded, and that amplified the inspirational dreams and constructive energies of Anton Seidl, Jeannette Thurber, and Henry Krehbiel.

(1993)

4 · *The Transcendental Ives*

Not long ago, a British musician of my acquaintance remarked the Leonard Bernstein should have studied conducting in Europe as a young man. This would have curbed certain interpretive eccentricities, my friend suggested. Bernstein would have more fully consummated his prodigious natural talent.

I disagree. To the extent that Bernstein was rooted in American jazz and popular song (he came relatively late to classical music), to the extent that his mentor Koussevitzky was devoted to American composers, Bernstein was able to forge a homegrown artistic personality more authentic than any hybrid that Old World tutelage could have fostered. In fact, it seems to me that the most significant North American concert and operatic performers have profited from a certain remoteness from European models. I am thinking of Glenn Gould, whose engrossing yet self-referential Bach achieved a heterodoxy more cocky and complete than any European's could be. Or of Jon Vickers, none of whose great roles sounded remotely idiomatic. Vickers's Otello could only have been diminished by closer contact with a Martinelli or Del Monaco. I have heard American singers more Italianate than Vickers in Italian roles, American pianists who evoke Schnabel or Horowitz with remarkable panache—and who will be forgotten while memories of Vickers and Gould remain.

American composers, too, run the gamut from imitation to eccentricity. The fullest polarization occurred around the turn of the twentieth century, when, compared to later decades, American creators could be closer to Europe or further away. Our Old World cultural parents were less distant in time—and so was an untrammeled New World, untouched by European worldliness. This was the time of Edward MacDowell and George Chadwick, whose formidable symphonic and chamber works reflected studies with Raff, Reinecke, and Rheinberger in Frankfurt, Leipzig, and Munich. And it was the time of Charles Edward Ives, who called his father—a sometime New England bandmaster—his principal teacher.

At Yale, it is true, Ives studied composition with Horatio Parker, who, like Chadwick, had studied composition with Rheinberger. But Parker and Ives viewed one another with a guarded respect; Ives later wrote: "Parker was a famous musician and a composer and Father wasn't a famous musician nor a composer, but I would say, of the two, Father was by far the greater man." Ives also identified with Ralph Waldo Emerson, who in 1837 had famously advised Americans: "Our day of dependence, our long apprenticeship to the learned of other lands, draws to a close. We will walk on our own feet; we will work with our own hands; we will speak our own minds." In the same breath, Emerson wrote: "I embrace the common, I explore and sit at the feet of the familiar, the low." Emerson's soulmate Henry David Thoreau, in a passage of which Ives was fond, echoed: "Natural objects and phenomena are the original symbols or types which express our thoughts and feelings, and yet American scholars, having little or no root in the soil, commonly strive with all their might to confine themselves to the imported symbols alone."

Ives drew inspiration from his father's world: from the Danbury, Connecticut, of his childhood; from the "common" and "familiar," "natural objects and pleasures," from chapel hymns and corny theater tunes. To a degree uncanny and extreme, the preserved memories of father and childhood anchored his creative identity—as did his surrogate Transcendentalist fathers, Emerson and Thoreau. Of all three of these fathers, two of whom he never met, Ives spoke with reverence and a peculiar familiarity. Long after George Ives died in 1894, Charles—in the words of his disciple John Kirkpatrick—"talked about his father as a personality. He lived . . . almost in a state of Chinese ancestor worship. He talked of his father as if he was still living, as if he were still a member of the household—it was that immediate." "He lived as though Emerson were standing beside him," adds the Ives scholar Vivian Perlis.

We too often think of Ives as a maverick, an anomaly, an outsider, explicable mainly in terms of idiosyncrasy. Ives was at the same time rooted in an older America. And it wasn't just the small Connecticut town in which he grew up.

Transcendentalism began in eastern Massachusetts in the 1830s as a reform movement within the Unitarian Church. Emerson, among other Transcendentalists, was himself a Unitarian minister. Denounced as "infidels" by conservative critics, Transcendentalists stressed the experience of individual inspiration. They disdained the harsh Puritan God of other American denominations. They espoused self-reliance, God in Nature, and social reform. Most Transcendentalists believed in the possibility of an intuitive identification with God, a Universal Intelligence (Thoreau's term) manifest in nature: a source of goodness.

Ives read and reread Emerson and Thoreau. He identified with them as people, as thinkers, and as stylists.

The unreined individualist in Emerson and Thoreau of course captivated Ives. "Ives aimed at the same spontaneity, the same freedom," Kirkpatrick recalled. "Emerson was a Yankee individualist—he didn't give a damn for the reactions of anybody." Parallel to his private career as a composer, Ives undertook a public vocation in life insurance. By middle age he was wealthy and successful. And yet he pursued a life-style as reclusive—as ostentatiously simple, in its way—as Thoreau's.

No less than Emerson or Thoreau, Ives was intensely democratic. He identified with the barber, the farmer, the country neighbor. He detested rank and caste. He celebrated the common man. The Transcendentalists, though solitary searchers, aspired to worldly influence through social experiments like Brook Farm. Ives, by comparison, was too much the loner to seek community. But he possessed a warm and meddlesome social conscience. Those who knew him testified to the generosity and kindliness underlying his fiercely laconic demeanor. His proposed Twentieth Amendment, which he circulated to leading political figures, would have implemented a national direct democracy.

Like Emerson and Thoreau, Ives was religious by temperament. He felt a kinship with the New England come-outers, who removed themselves from institutions that violated their conscience. Thoreau's abolitionism and civil disobedience are offshoots of this tradition. Ives's Christianity was less heretical, but he was far from an orthodox worshiper. ("Many of the sincerest followers of Christ," he once wrote, "never heard of him.") He followed Emerson and Thoreau in his religious regard for nature, in his conviction that the world is a wholesome place, in his insistence that art, like nature, is moral. Ives aspired to the condition—immortalized by Thoreau in *Walden*—where art, religion, philosophy, and daily life become one and the same. Among the advertisements he wrote for the firm of Ives and Myrick was one beginning:

> "I appeal from your customs: I must be myself"—says Emerson in his "Self-Reliance."
>
> There is a tendency, today, to minimize the individual and to exaggerate the machinelike custom of business and of life.
>
> Some men fit quite easily into a mechanistic system, while others feel that their individuality will be or is being gradually standardized out of them.
>
> Work in the life insurance field certainly doesn't cramp

individuality, ingenuity or initiative. Men of character, who are capable of sustained hard work, who like to overcome obstacles, who are interested in human nature, may well consider the profession of life insurance.

On his business associates Ives impressed the belief that life insurance was humanitarian. The composer Lou Harrison attributed to Ives—both the man and his music—the idea of "inclusivity— that you don't do exclusively one kind of thing."

Harrison met Ives only in 1947, when Ives was old and infirm.

> The first thing I encountered was Mr. Ives waving a cane so vigorously in a whirling fashion that I was quite frightened. He was shouting, "My old friend! My old friend!" and I had never seen the man before in my life! Then he greeted me, so grandly, so enthusiastically. I almost expected to find him incapacitated, and was quite taken back to discover myself ducking from a cane. He literally danced, he got so excited.

To Harrison, Ives at seventy-two "looked like God the Father as done by William Blake." The poet Louis Untermeyer visited Ives about three years before and testified: "He knew what he had done. He knew what he was, and that was that. He took it for granted and I took it for granted. . . . I have had that with a few people only. Robert Frost was one. He had that quality too. I felt it immediately with Ives."

Ives was an Everyman who cherished the quotidian, a vigorous democrat addicted to ordinary people and things. He was a charismatic philosopher who idealized art and spiritualized everyday experience. His music is equally prone to plain and extravagant speech. These juxtapositions, if contradictory, are not singular, but quintessential Emerson, quintessential Thoreau.

The Transcendentalist writings of Emerson and Thoreau are packed with metaphor. Using nature as a symbol for spiritual illumination, the authors "cast a poetic veil" (Emerson's phrase) over the experiences they found most sacred. Literal meanings are elusive or misleading. The ecstatic "music" of their poetry and prose transcends rational exegesis. The music of Ives likewise abounds in metaphor and symbolism: images of rural play, philosophy culled from wanderings and books. Its ecstasies are obscure and religious. Like Emerson's prose, it violates orthodoxies of grammar, of harmony and form. Though its dissonance and "difficulty" parallel the new language of Schoenberg an ocean away (and although Schoenberg came to admire Ives), Ives did not know the music of Schoenberg and other turn-of-the-century European innovators. His stubborn self-sufficiency dictated a singular isolation from mainstream "classical music." "Listening to concert music seemed to confuse me in my own work . . . to throw me off from what I had in mind," he later wrote. Nor did Ives hear his own music; for decades it lay unperformed. He irritably shunned the company and even the approbation of "celebrated musicians."

The interior vision into which Ives withdrew was nourished by George Ives's sound world of hymns, marches, and Civil War songs—a world equally divorced from European high culture and its American parlor parody. The second wellspring was Transcendentalism: its inherent music of the mind and senses.

In their landmark *Charles Ives and His Music* (1955), Henry and Sidney Cowell observed of Ives's isolation that it "increased his concentration upon the music of the Idea, of the Transcendental, music that was uninhibited by the limitations of people and instruments, satisfying to the composer even if unheard." The same could be said of the deaf Beethoven. And Ives in fact likened Thoreau to Beethoven, who in his deafness knew the "religion of contemplation": "The rhythm of [Thoreau's] prose, were there nothing else, would determine his value as a composer. He was divinely conscious of the enthusiasm of Nature, the motion of her rhythms and the harmony of her solitude. . . . In their greatest moments the inspiration of both Beethoven and Thoreau express profound truths and deep sentiment." Thoreau himself said of music: "Our minds should echo at least as many times as a Mammoth Cave to every musical sound. It should awaken reflections in us." Thoreau also wrote: "I wish to hear the silence of the night, for the silence is something positive and to be heard. . . . A fertile and eloquent silence. . . . Silence alone is worthy to be heard. . . . The silence rings; it is musical and thrills me."

Thoreau played his flute in rural solitude. In the "Thoreau" movement of his *Concord* Sonata (1911–15), Ives asks that a flute be played. In fact, Ives's essay "Thoreau" sketches a program for his composition "Thoreau." Thoreau sits in his doorway at Walden, "rapt in revery, amidst goldenrod, sandcherry and sumach." Though "he realized what the Oriental meant by Contemplation and forsaking of works," he does not contemplate in this style. Ives, accordingly, does not imitate Eastern music: "Thus it is not the whole tone scale of the Orient but the scale of the Walden morning which inspired many of the polyphonies and harmonies that come to us through his poetry." And Ives's gently rippling music—barless, fragmentary, transparent—does evoke the early morning's fluttering of leaves and wind—and also the fluttering of half-formulated early morning thoughts. In "The Housatonic at Stockbridge," from *Three Places in New England,* Ives's plucked harp tones, and trembling and oscillating strings, fashion an incorporeal sonic landscape, all *pp* and *pppp:* the "thrilling music" of Thoreau's silence; a Transcendental ether, physically and metaphysically aquiver; a half-heard, half-seen aureole crowning mist, water, and floating leaves.

Ives's essay "Emerson" again incorporates musical metaphor and allusion. Sentence upon sentence equally describes Emerson and Ives, words and notes:

> To think hard and deeply and to say what is thought, regardless of consequences, may produce a first impression, either of great translucence, or of great muddiness, but in the latter there may be hidden possibilities. Some accuse Brahms' orchestration of being muddy. . . . But if it

should seem less so, he might not be saying what he thought. . . . A clearer scoring might have lowered the thought.

Here is Emerson, in his poem "Music:"

> 'Tis not in the high stars alone,
> Nor in the cup of budding flowers,
> Nor in the redbreast's mellow tone,
> Nor in the bow that smiles in showers,
> But in the mud and scum of things
> There alway, alway something sings.

Pursuing "the scum of things," Ives the composer constructs a cacophony of American life, piling layer upon dissonant layer of noise and song: overlapping bands, church hymns jostling with boyhood revels. In his religious mode, he improvises freely, unconstrained by rule or tradition. Writing of Emerson, he contends: "Vagueness is at times an indication of nearness to a perfect truth. . . . Orderly reason does not always have to be a visible part of all great things."

Probably the best-loved image of Ives the iconoclast, striding far ahead of his time and place, is of Ives the haranguer, shouting "Sissy!" and "Listen like a man!" at obtuse contemporaries. But this is a calumny, perpetuated by many who write about Ives; it reveals at least as much about Ives as about his milieu.

Whatever truth adheres to Ives's characterization of effete artists and culture-bearers, he was—again—living less in the future than in the past. He was remembering the New England parlor of his childhood and shutting out the New York of his mature years. In contrast to conservative Boston, turn-of-the-century New York was a world cultural metropolis. Fifteen years before, James Gibbons Huneker, arriving from Philadelphia, had poked around and discovered Ambrose Bierce and Emma Goldman, anarchists and Nietzscheans. Anton Seidl and his unsurpassed German ensemble at the Metropolitan Opera delivered the orgasmic jolts of *Götterdämmerung* and *Tristan und Isolde* with a shocking veracity. By the decade of the 1910s, when Ives was at his creative peak, New York–based critics such as Carl Van Vechten and Paul Rosenfeld, New York–based composers such as Leo Ornstein and Edgard Varèse were committed modernists. This was also the period of Frank Lloyd Wright, John Marin, Alfred Stieglitz, Isadora Duncan, Carl Sandburg, Ezra Pound.

Ives, living in Manhattan, made contact with none of these composers, writers, and visual artists. His life-style was that of a proper businessman. He was discomfited by sensuality. He denounced homosexuals as "pansies," "lily-pads," "old ladies," "pussy-boys." He disliked the company of bohemians. His disdain for the feminized Connecticut culture he recalled was exacerbated by knowledge of his own complicity. He feared his sentimentality. His songs, his First Symphony both incorporate and critique the genteel. He was prone to denounce as "effeminate" sensual and aestheticist tendencies that actually threatened the genteel tradition.

In some ways, the contemporary American musician Ives most revealingly evokes is the conductor Theodore Thomas. At first the analogy seems preposterous. Thomas was upright. He repudiated popular music. His repertoire stopped with Bruckner, Sibelius, and Richard Strauss. But Thomas, too, was a prepossessing autodidact, self-made and self-reliant. He was caustic and pugnacious. Touring the United States with his Thomas Orchestra, he beat the pulpit for Beethoven and Brahms. He called his concerts "sermons in tones." A pioneer in the wilderness, he exuded moral fervor. No less than Ives—or Emerson, or Thoreau—he was religious by temperament, an optimist, and a democrat. Finally, in compensation for prevailing stereotypes of artists and musicians, he conspicuously embodied an exaggerated masculinity. He was athletic. He disapproved of eccentricities of dress and demeanor. He looked like a banker.

Thomas wielded great influence as the father of the American concert orchestra. He attained his peak popularity during Ives's Danbury years. But by the time Ives came to New York in 1898, Thomas was an anachronism, at least by New York standards. Seidl, by comparison, was inscrutable and Romantic: an *artiste.* "Effeminacy" was no longer an issue—yet it remained so for Ives.

If these remarks simplify or distort the complexities of Ives as man and artist, they reinforce his devotion to an earlier world, buoyed by Transcendental security and optimism.

In 1918 Ives suffered a severe breakdown*. Within a few years he had virtually given up composing. Ives the businessman retreated to semiretirement. His social isolation increased. His devoted wife, Harmony, nursed him as he declined into illness. He died at the age of seventy-nine in 1954.

The belated discovery of Ives the composer began fitfully in the 1920s. Henry Cowell emerged as Ives's most influential champion. With the coming of the 1930s a more propitious aesthetic climate congealed: intellectuals who had rebelled against American provincialism a decade earlier now located a usable past among the New England writers Ives had so used; a more sanguine, more patriotic tone prevailed. Nicolas Slonimsky's premiere performance of *Three Places in New England,* at Town Hall in 1931 (seventeen years after its composition), was a landmark in Ives's emergence. So, in 1932, was the performance of seven Ives songs at the First Festival of Contemporary American Music at Yaddo, organized by Aaron Copland. When in 1939 John Kirkpatrick gave the New York premiere of the *Concord* Sonata, Law-

---

*According to most sources, a heart attack. But Stuart Feder, in his 1993 psychoanalytical biography *Charles Ives: "My Father's Song,"* has questioned this received wisdom. Ives and his wife may not have meant "heart attack" in the modern sense of "coronary thrombosis," but rather a subjective experience of severe anxiety with attendant rapid heart rate. Feder's review of existing medical records fails to confirm symptoms of myocardial infarction.

rence Gilman's review in the *New York Herald Tribune* conveyed an unprecedented mainstream imprimatur:

> This sonata is exceptionally great music—it is, indeed, the greatest music composed by an American, and the most deeply and essentially American in impulse and implication. It is wide-ranging and capacious. It has passion, tenderness, humor, simplicity, homeliness. It has imaginative and spiritual vastness. It has wisdom and beauty and profundity, and a sense of the encompassing terror and splendor of human life and human destiny—a sense of those mysteries that are both human and divine.

Ives was now hailed as a veritable modernist or proto-modernist, a discoverer, with Schoenberg, of new tonal worlds. But Ives's putative modernism was an accident or paradox. When Paul Rosenfeld, in 1933, found Ives's appropriation of patriotic songs "savagely sardonic," he reconstructed Ives's unreconstructed worldview; Ives loved those old tunes. And Copland, the leader of America's composers' community, was, again, of another world: he could never have followed Ives into Emerson's "mud and scum of things" in search of spiritual ecstasies.

In fact, the phenomenon Ives is unthinkable after World War I. Ives essentially predates cosmopolitan modernism. He essentially predates the Great War, with its economic and spiritual rupture from past American experience. He predates the influx of refugee artists and intellectuals, who deflected the quest for an indigenous American voice. Devoted to the world of his fathers, he actually predates urban America. In secluded retirement, he railed against the movies, the radio, the telephone, popular music, and the automobile. Frank R. Rossiter, in his indispensable *Charles Ives and His America* (1975), shrewdly remarks:

> Much of [Ives's] dissatisfaction with American life in [the 1920s] arose from his feeling that the new mass culture

was throwing off the genteel restraints of the past. . . .
Combining his gentility with his tendency to place art on
a pedestal, high above the mundane and trivial, Ives
greeted this extraordinarily rich decade in American culture with a rhetorical question: "Is it better to sing inade-
quately of the 'leaf on Walden floating,' and die 'dead but
not dishonored,' or to sing adequately of the 'cherry on the
cocktail,' and live forever?"

Ives would not read newspapers. On one occasion in the 1930s,
Slonimsky discovered that Ives was unaware of Roosevelt's reelec-
tion. The coming of Hitler seemed simply unacceptable to Ives:
"Why doesn't somebody do something about it?!" he would thunder, or withdraw into silence. His willful ignorance of worldly
events was a form of self-protection. He clung to his Transcendental faith in progress and human goodness. When, late in life, he
revisited Danbury with his nephew Bigelow Ives, he moaned
aloud to see how much had changed. All his life, he kept such
mementos as a football, knee pants, baseballs, and spiked shoes.

Ives the progressive needed to live in the past. That is why, in
his music, we recognize him not only as American but also—perhaps more than any other composer—as an emblematic American, speaking for us all because speaking of origins. It is why he
seems at once maverick and familiar.

(1994)

5 · *Mahler, Klimt, and Fin de Siècle Vienna*

Not since the death of Beethoven had Vienna seen a funeral as splendid as Johannes Brahms's. Spanish standard-bearers and torch-bearers accompanied the hearse. So many flowers followed that the cortege was said to resemble "a gigantic moving garden." The streets were filled with people, as were vantage points on houses lining the route. The procession stopped at the Vienna Philharmonic Society, where black cloth draped the buildings and blue flames flickered in suspended bowls; members of the Singverein performed the partsong "Fahr wohl." Another sung tribute took place at the gravesite, where Beethoven and Schubert were already interred.

Eduard Hanslick, the *éminence grise* among Viennese music critics, considered Brahms to be Beethoven's heir; fellow Brahmsians called Brahms's First Symphony Beethoven's Tenth. Brahms's enemies were said to be Berlioz, Liszt, Wagner, Bruckner, and Wolf, whose supporters returned the Hanslick camp's hostility. In retrospect, Brahms was a mighty anachronism by the time he died in 1897; his resplendent cortege symbolized the passing of an era. Berlioz, Liszt, Wagner, and Bruckner were already gone. Wolf was confined to an insane assylum in September 1897—some five months after Brahms's death. Gustav Mahler now became Vienna's leading musical progressive.

Brahms, who drily called Mahler "king of the revolutionaries," had enjoyed the younger man's periodic visits; Mahler, for his part, felt respect and tolerant affection for the crusty master. In fact, Vienna's high-culture milieu was notably integrated and compact. More than London's, Paris's, or Berlin's, its intellectuals and artists, scholars and journalists, politicians and doctors knew one another. Their professional communities overlapped, spilling into the same cafés and salons. The symbolism of 1897 spills into painting, sculpture, handicrafts, and architecture: the year Brahms died, a youthful generation of dissident Viennese artists formed the "Secession." Its motto was "To the Age Its Art, to Art Its Freedom." Its effect was to open Austria to European innovations in the visual arts, especially to art nouveau. To the degree Brahms had been a Viennese symbol of tradition, the Secession symbolized revolt.

Mahler was thirty-seven in 1897. The leading Secessionist, Gustav Klimt, was thirty-five. In fin de siècle Vienna, their rebelliousness forecast the expressionism of Arnold Schoenberg and Oskar Kokoschka, ages twenty-three and eleven in 1897. The evolution from Mahler to Schoenberg encapsulates a phased response to spent Romanticism; so does the evolution from Klimt to Kokoschka. The tight weave of Viennese high culture additionally suggests interdisciplinary linkages between Mahler and Klimt, Schoenberg and Kokoschka. In ways surprising and obvious, Viennese music and painting illuminate one another.

The year that Brahms died and the Secession was born was triply significant for the arts in Vienna: Mahler was named director of the Opera in 1897. Overnight, he transformed the cultural hub of the "city of music." In the pit he conducted, it was said, with the excitability of "an epileptic cat." Behind the scenes he was a brazen, idealistic administrator. His innovations included removing the claque, closing the doors to latecomers, and lowering the pit. His principal designer, Alfred Roller, overthrew canons of verisimilitude. Roller's first production, in 1903, was a new *Tris-*

tan und Isolde. Stressing symbolism over naturalism, he assigned color motifs to each act: orange-red flared from the sails and curtains of Marke's ship; violet-blue suffused the *Liebesnacht;* cold gray lit the dying Tristan. "The conception of the music of light," the critic Oscar Bie called it. Roller's costumes were in the art nouveau style of the Secession, of which he was a founding member.

A second important link from Mahler to the Secession was Alma Schindler, his wife as of 1902. Her father taught the Secessionist painter Carl Moll, later her stepfather. (The critic Hermann Bahr, once Hugo Wolf's roommate, likened Moll's paintings to Schubert's songs.) Alma Mahler wore dresses and jewelry by Kolo Moser and Josef Hoffmann of the Secessionist Wiener Werkstätte. She was also friendly with Klimt, who had once been in love with her. From the time of his marriage Mahler, too, knew Klimt well. When in 1902 Klimt unveiled his Beethoven frieze, representing the Ninth Symphony, Mahler appeared to conduct a passage from the finale in his own arrangement for winds.

In his landmark *Fin-de-Siècle Vienna: Politics and Culture* (1980), Carl Schorske characterizes Vienna's "new culture makers" as mounting a "collective Oedipal revolt." For the Secessionists, the rejected father figures included the painter Hans Makart, whose realism dictated taste at the Imperial Academy. At the same time, *Die Junge* did not spurn the past as thoroughly as later modernists would. Schorske sees them making "critical reformulations or subversive transformations of their traditions." This was Mahler's way at the Opera, where rethinkings of Mozart and Beethoven were among his highest achievements. In *Don Giovanni* Roller's stylized sets promoted instantaneous scene changes, promoting in turn a unified musical-dramatic flow. Mahler commissioned a new German translation of the libretto. "Again," comments Kurt Blaukopf in his Mahler biography (1973), "he was not out to make changes at any cost. Passages of the text which by their popularity had become an integral part of the work were allowed to remain unmodified, but where musical logic or dramatic consistency was violated, the changes came in." And Mahler eliminated customary top notes, cadenzas, and appoggiaturas; rather than "authenticity," he sought a timely Mozart style counteracting rococo prettiness and divisive vocal display. The same logic—aiming to reconnect with abused tradition while expunging traditional abuse—moved him to alter the scoring in *Fidelio* and other Beethoven works, accounting for the differences between modern instruments and those Beethoven knew.

More enduring than Mahler's operatic reforms, however, is his legacy as a composer—in which capacity he was controversial in fin de siècle Vienna, but much less known than today. Here again Mahler's achievement complexly combines tradition and change. As a tonal symphonist, he sustained the lineage of Beethoven and Brahms. But the sung texts, temperamental extremes, and sheer length of Mahler's symphonies connected to Wagnerian Music of the Future; his first three symphonies (1888–95) are actually programmatic. To conservative critics of Mahler's time, this post-Romantic, post-Wagnerian dimension was enough to make Mahler an irredeemable wild man, pursuing with neurotic intensity primal feelings and metaphysical themes desecrating symphonic decorum. This aspect of Mahler's status as a fin de siècle fulcrum—his way of cramming a Romantic chaos of emotion and intellectual quest into the traditional Classical forms—was not his chief aesthetic heresy, however. Newer and more truly controversial were deeper strains of seeming self-contradiction. As Henry Krehbiel, the dean of New York music critics during Mahler's years with the Metropolitan Opera and New York Philharmonic (1908–11), wrote in his Mahler obituary of May 21, 1911:

It was a singular paradox in Mahler's artistic nature that while his melodic ideas were of the folksong order his treatment of them was of the most extravagant kind, harmonically and orchestrally. He attempted in argument to reconcile the extremes by insisting that folksong was the vital spark of artistic music, but in his treatment of the simple melodies of his symphonies . . . he was utterly inconsiderate of their essence, robbing them of their characteristics and elaborating them to death. . . . We cannot see how any of his music can long survive him. There is no place for it between the old and the new schools.

This naked juxtaposition of vernacular and "serious" elements, placing Mahler's symphonies "between the old and new schools," was something really new—puzzling, tantalizing, infuriating, illuminating. Compared to *Tristan*'s self-revealing reveries and rantings, Mahler's "stream of consciousness" was Freudian: a mélange of high tragedy and commonplace detail, of elation and pratfall. As is well known, Mahler consulted Freud in 1910 and fixed upon a childhood memory: how once, during a violent scene between his parents, he rushed from the house and heard an organ grinder's popular ditty ("Ach, du lieber Augustin"). This juxtaposition, Mahler came to believe, was so fixed in his memory that in his own music the noblest passages were "spoiled" by prosaic intrusions. On another occasion, writing to Bruno Walter, Mahler said of his Third Symphony:

I have no doubt that our friends the critics . . . will once again suffer from dizziness. . . . The whole thing is . . . tainted with my deplorable sense of humor. . . . It is well known that I cannot do without trivialities. This time, however, all permissible bounds have been passed. "One often feels that one has got into a pub or pigsty!"

Though Krehbiel bristled at Mahlerian "paradox," drastic inconsistencies of idiom and mood are what generate the disturbing tensions and liberating ambiguities that keep Mahler's music vital seven decades after his death. In an appreciative 1941 commentary, Ernst Krenek cited the Third Symphony's posthorn—whose catchy tune resembles a popular song—and observed:

> The material is neither novel nor original. The striking boldness of this and many similar passages lies in the fact that such apparently commonplace associations are used with the will to give voice to deep emotion and profound philosophical thought. The result is obtained by choosing first an obviously outworn, obsolete symbol, so that it appears as a quotation from another age and style, and by then placing it in a surprising context of grandeur and monumentality.
>
> Seen from this angle, Mahler's style anticipates the basic principle of surrealism to an amazing extent. Doubtless Mahler was conscious of the extra-musical associations attached to many of his themes: children's songs, folk tunes, country dances, bugle calls, army marches, and so forth. However, the associations never function according to the schedule of an extra-musical program, as they did in the symphonic poem of the Liszt and Strauss school. They function by their contrast to the immense symphonic context in which they appear. The opening motive of the Third Symphony is literally identical with the first phrase of a marching song which all Austrian school-children used to sing. Produced by eight French horns playing at full blast in unison and placed in empty space, without any accompaniment, at the beginning of a symphonic movement of unheard-of dimensions, this motive takes on a very special significance precisely because of its being associated with that innocent little tune; a significance, however, that it would be difficult to analyze.

Other prescient Mahlerian pastiches evoke Ives's cacophonous fairgrounds or certain *Neue Sachlichkeit* strategies of Hindemith and Weill or, more generally, the fascination with the banal as a twentieth-century antidote to suffocating Romantic inwardness.

In the context of Viennese generational conflict and change, Mahler, director of the Opera, and Klimt, first president of the Secession, were friends and contemporaries, disobedient sons and influential fathers. As conductor and composer, Mahler was a fulcrum figure. So was Klimt. As Kirk Varnedoe comments in his 1986 catalogue essay for the Museum of Modern Art's "Vienna 1900":

> At the turn of the century, Klimt embodied both authority and rebellion. . . . After Makart's death Klimt, regarded as his "heir," became a favored painter for the ceilings of the later Ringstrasse buildings. As an honored young professor, Klimt thus commanded special respect, in the 1890s, from forward-looking artists' clubs like the Siebener (the Seven) of Josef Hoffmann and Koloman Moser. But as an aging prodigy who had spent too many hours on scaffolds satisfying institutional tastes . . . he was ripe to be converted to their idea that modern art had something better to offer.

Klimt's receptivity to heterodox currents was, like Mahler's, partly temperamental. Like Mahler, he favored a psychological realism stressing desire and anxiety, neurosis and transcendence. Like Mahler, again, he kept one foot in the past, addressing the future sporadically, contradictorily, ambiguously.

Klimt's panel *Music* (1898), for a private music salon, is a case in point. As Schorske explains in his *Fin-de-Siècle Vienna,* a songstress appears beside two stone figures: "Silenus, the companion of Dionysus, whom Nietzsche called 'a symbol of the sexual omnipotence of nature,'" and the Sphinx, "embodiment of the metamorphic continuum of animal and man, of terror and female beauty." Silenus and the Sphinx "seem to represent the buried instinctual forces which the Apollonian necromancer will summon in song." Klimt's three figures symbolize music's power to excavate unruly instinct—yet their reportorial, almost photographic rendering is startlingly disciplined and direct. A further dissonance is the decorative, two-dimensional background—including, somehow, the songstress's stylized lyre. As Varnedoe pertinently comments, in discussing other realistic-symbolic Klimts of this period, the "underlying realism produce[s] an uncomfortable immediacy, as if idealist visions [are] being staged as costumed tableaux vivants." Like Mahler's, Klimt's "inconsistencies"—his hybridization of tone and idiom—catalyze an aroused, inquisitive response.

Around the same time that he painted *Music,* Klimt began work on a public commission: three allegorical ceiling murals for the University of Vienna, representing Philosophy, Medicine, and Jurisprudence. The story of these controversial paintings, which were lost to fire during World War II but survive in photographs, further illuminates the tensions between Klimt and nineteenth-century tradition, and within Klimt's work itself. *Philosophy* (1900) shows a tangle of naked bodies floating aimlessly in a viscous void; eighty-seven faculty members signed a petition asking the Ministry of Culture to reject its "unclear" ideas and forms. *Medicine* (1901) offers another mass of drifting bodies, including a pregnant woman and a woman with her pelvis thrust forward. Characteristically merging symbolism and naturalism, Klimt does not idealize these nudes; his critics found *Medicine* "indecent."

Potentially more gripping or unsettling than the obscure symbolism and unclothed anatomies of *Philosophy* and *Medicine,* however, is the anti-Enlightened worldview conveyed by the aqueous cosmos they inhabit, with its passage of floating, torpid humanity (the elements of Klimt's third ceiling painting, *Jurisprudence,* are more "stable"). Schorske, describing *Medicine,* sees "a phantasmagoria of half-dreaming humanity, sunk in instinctual semi-surrender, passive in the flow of fate." As in other Klimt paintings, the liquefied medium suggests a stratum of primal subjectivity, an unconscious world of instinct dissolving every "I," a fatalistic vision of transient humanity more Eastern than Western. More specifically, suggests Schorske, "Klimt's vision of the universe is Schopenhauer's—the world as Will, as blind energy in an endless round of meaningless parturience, love, and death."

Inferring Zarathustra's "Drunken Song of Midnight" as the psychological and philosophical subtext of *Philosophy,* Schorske creates a bridge between Klimt and Mahler, whose setting of the same Nietzsche poem is the centerpiece of his Third Symphony (1895). This is an inspired analogy, and not merely because Mahler was a student of Schopenhauer's theory of music (as an immediate manifestation of the Will). Imagine Klimt's entangled bodies rising, falling, tumbling in slow motion, and apply the music and text of Mahler's "O Mensch! Gib acht," and you will arrive at an eerie synthesis.

To glimpse this vision of mankind cosmically afloat is to experience a Mahler emotional signature, an ambience of ego dispersion at once sensuous, resigned, morbid, comforting. In fact, Klimt's imagery of particles drifting in an aqueous void is made palpable in Mahler's music, and without the mediation of words. Plucked (not strummed) harp tones are one Mahlerian rendering of universal particles endlessly afloat. The Fifth Symphony's familiar *Adagietto* (1902) is punctuated nearly throughout by harp tones whose gently irregular rhythm suggests aquatic flux; it is the "water music" of Visconti's film *Death in Venice,* after Thomas Mann's sensuous, resigned novella.

More obviously metaphysical is Mahler's treatment of the harp in the "Abschied" from *Das Lied von der Erde* (1908). The slowly oscillating plucked thirds first appear at the words "Der Bach singt voller Wohllaut durch das Dunkel [The brook sings, full of melody, through the darkness]." But the water here is metaphoric, gently, sensuously propelling a resigned farewell to life. In Mahler's Ninth Symphony (1909), also a leave-taking, harp tones articulate the slow motion of both outer movements. The oscillating thirds of the harp's final appearance (m. 88) occupy a void: the absence of a bass line parallels the groundlessness of Klimt's visual field, which shows bodies drifting in and out of the frame. Mahler and Klimt dissolve the boundaries of what is seen and heard, blur distinctions between the "I" and the world, being and nonbeing.

What brings the analogy between Mahler and fin de siècle visual arts most sharply into focus, finally, is decoration. In art nouveau (of which the Secession was the Austrian equivalent), decorative elements became autonomous. Rebelling against academic art, art nouveau rebelled against the hierarchical precedence of fine arts over applied, with its ivory tower implications. Liberated from subservience to contextual representation or meaning, the use of line attained an independent importance predicated on sheer visual appeal.

In Vienna, the Wiener Werkstätte was the Secession's art-and-crafts workshop, a source of carpets and upholstery, dishes and utensils. In 1904 Klimt joined the Wiener Werkstätte artists in designing a villa in Brussels, the Stoclet House. Long before, however, he had received an artisan's training from his father, a goldsmith. Klimt's feeling for design was a constant feature of his output; multicolored patterns of decorative motifs are a Klimt trademark. Especially during his "gold" period (1906–9), Klimt's vibrant, meticulous decorative patterns, highlighted by applications of gold leaf, challenge or overwhelm the figural content of his paintings. In *The Kiss* (1907–8), perhaps his best-known work, only the heads, arms, hands, and feet of the lovers are rendered in three dimensions; the rest of the canvas is swallowed up by variegated two-dimensional decoration, much of it gold. Flatness and depth, foreground and background, fantasy and reality oscillate stroboscopically. In Klimt's portrait *Adele Bloch-Bauer I* (1907), the human figure is even more obsessively dissolved into legato spirals and staccato rectangles and triangles, a vocabulary of interlocking geometric and biological forms prominently including stacked "Egyptian" eyes. The Stoclet frieze, executed by the Wiener Werkstätte (1911) from Klimt's designs (1905–9), maximizes

In *The Kiss* (1907–8), perhaps Klimt's best-known work, two-dimensional decoration overwhelms the three-dimensional figural content. Collection: Osterreichisches Galerie, Vienna, Austria. Used by permission.

the decorative component, with its roots in archaic forms. Varnedoe writes:

> In the archaic splendor of their irregular relief and gemlike colors, these panels defined a modern Byzantium. . . . Nowhere are the tensions in Klimt's art—between representation and abstraction, between high art and artisanry, between the dreamlike and the concrete—more powerfully

The human figure is even more dissolved into legato spirals and staccato rectangles in *Portrait of Adele Bloch-Bauer I* (1907). Collection: Osterreichisches Galerie, Vienna, Austria. Used by permission.

exercised than in the obsessive, whorling brilliance of this celebration of love as fusion and dissolution.

The descriptive vocabulary elicited by fin de siècle decorative patterning—"line," "rhythm," "cadence"—is inescapably musical; Varnedoe even calls the Wiener Werkstätte designs, with their ingeniously balanced, richly varied colors and materials, a "tour de force of symphonic orchestration." In Mahler, autonomous decoration—ingeniously balanced, richly varied—is a tour de force;

no prior symphonist so stresses the sheer aural appeal of discrete ornamental detail. Even Klimt's use of gold finds an analogy in the delicate "metalwork" wrought by Mahler's triangles, cymbals, bells, gongs, harps, glockenspiels, tambourines, and celestas. Frequently, these are no mere color-dabs, but ongoing autonomous motifs. The jangling cowbells of the Sixth Symphony (1904), as unrelated to the surrounding rhythms and tunes as Klimt's gold leaf is unrelated to figurative content, connote Alpine "thin air." The pulsating sleighbells of the Fourth Symphony (1900) connote seraphic innocence; like Klimt's, Mahler's usage refers back to Byzantine mosaics, with their inlaid golden halos.

In fact, meticulous, multicolored ornamental designs are as much a trademark of Mahler as of Klimt. Like the intrusion of "mere" decoration in fin de siècle painting, the decorative component of Mahler's symphonic canvases was innovative, perplexing, controversial. Reviewing the 1889 premiere of Mahler's First (1888), a newspaper critic wrote: "The thematic working is too often pushed into the background at the expense of coloristic effect, and there are certain empty passages: color without design"—that is, decoration divorced from symphonic structure. Mahler himself, describing the second movement of his Fourth Symphony (1900), said: "Often the thousand little fragments of the picture change so kaleidoscopically that it's impossible to recognize it again." The movement in question is a slowly spinning scherzo propelled by the constant variation of overlapping motivic cells, a rotating kaleidoscope whose tumbling, jostling particles of colored sand ceaselessly reconfigure. At every point the field of vision fills with engrossing surface detail. The tactile precision of every bleating, trilling, crowing, chattering motif (the score teems with details of articulation, phrasing, dynamics) negates distinctions between foreground and background. Like Klimt's decorative swaths, Mahler's sound mosaics are relatively two-dimensional. In the first movement of the Fourth Symphony, the same techniques generate a sonata form: the expansive principal themes are fragmented, superimposed, recombined.

Aligned with Mahler's new stress on decoration was a new use of the orchestra, an "emancipation from the piano" as a compositional aid. Progressing toward his middle symphonies, Mahler overthrew the convention of recessed, dependent woodwinds and brasses; he brought the winds forward into a complex web of distinct instrumental lines irreducible to keyboard textures. Of his Fifth Symphony (1902) he said: "The individual parts are so difficult to play that they all really need soloists. Some pretty bold passages and figures escaped me here, just because I do know the orchestra and its instruments so well." More often than not, Mahler employs his huge forces not to achieve volume and weight or a Straussian impasto of glitter and noisy energy, but to maximize clarity and contrast by means of unusual instrumental juxtapositions and combinations. While walking in the woods in 1900 he came upon a county fair spewing barrel organs, a male choir, a military band. According to a much-cited account, he exclaimed:

> Do you hear that? That's polyphony—and that's where I got it from. . . . That is how—for a lot of different sources—the themes must come, and like this they must be entirely different from each other in rhythm and melody—anything else is only part-writing and disguised homophony. What the artist has to do is organize them into an intelligible whole.

Klimt's polyphony combines archaic artisan motifs whose origins include Egyptian, Celtic, and Mycenean iconography. Mahler's polyphonic motifs move from rude military bands (trumpets and drums) to birdcall filigree (woodwinds) to spare, "oriental" renderings of water (harp). In pages such as the one reproduced opposite, from the Seventh Symphony's *Nachtmusik I* (1905), the complex of pithy nature sounds even visually evokes Klimtian decoration; like figurative elements in the Stoclet frieze, a superimposed tune in quarter notes (trumpets, trombones, solo violin, and double basses) bears a tenuous relationship to the surrounding

ornamental mosaic. Ludwig Hevesi, a leading fin de siècle art critic, found in Klimt's decorative patterning a metaphor for "never-ending, infinitely mutating primal matter—spinning, whirling, coiling, winding, twisting"—an apt description of the *Nachtmusik* passage, with its busy superimposed Ur forms.

The symbolism of Vienna 1897—of Brahms's death, Mahler's appointment, and the founding of the Secession—was also political. In 1897 Karl Lueger, who raged against Jews and capitalists, became Vienna's mayor. Eighteen ninety-seven was the year of the liberals' decisive defeat, of the dissolution of the Reichsrat and rule by decree. And it was the year that Theodor Herzl convened the First Zionist Congress, with its plan for a Jewish state. Vienna's antiliberal political culture—of mass movements in rebellion against reason and the law—left Austria polarized with regard to Jewish rights, Czech nationalism, Pan-Germanism. The anachronistic empire—a polyglot autocracy of Germans and Slavs, Catholics and Jews—was visibly being tugged apart. Vienna's traditional world of titled aristocrats, public pomp, and high culture had become a world of instability, contradiction, disintegration.

Instability, contradiction, disintegration are stylistic hallmarks of Mahler and Klimt. Fulcrum figures, they embody sons and fathers, past and future, representation and abstraction, Romantic and modern. "Infinitely mutating," their discourse fosters ambiguity, tension, critical distance.

Arnold Schoenberg wrote to Mahler in 1904 in praise of the latter's Third Symphony:

> I saw your very soul, naked, stark naked. It was revealed to me as a stretch of wild and secret country, with eerie chasms and abysses neighbored by sunlit, smiling meadows, haunts of idyllic repose. I felt [your symphony] as an event of nature which, after scouring us with its terrors, puts a rainbow in the sky. . . . I shared in the battling for illusion; I suffered the pangs of disillusionment; I saw the

forces of evil and good wrestling with each other; I saw a man in torment struggling for inner harmony; I divined a personality, a drama, and truthfulness, the most uncompromising truthfulness.

I had to let myself go. Forgive me. I cannot feel by halves. With me it is one thing or the other.

Schoenberg's letter, signed "in all devotion," is a filial homage; Schoenberg was later to call Mahler a "great man," "martyr," "saint." At the same time, the letter discloses the distance between Mahler's "foot in the past" and Schoenberg's leap into the future. Schoenberg's characterization of Mahler's Third ignores its instabilities of tone and perspective; he reads Mahler as an unbridled subjectivist—as an expressionist. In Schoenberg's expressionism—in his free atonal period, 1908 to 1913—there is not, as in Mahler, the justaposition of tradition and change, "serious" and vernacular, structure and "decoration." In such music as the nightmarish *Erwartung* (1909), Schoenberg's total chromaticism coexists with total, unmediated interiority. Mahler, who wrote nine symphonies and directed the Vienna Opera for a decade, was alienated by half; Schoenberg, by comparison, seemed to himself and to others a complete outsider.

With Schoenberg, it was "one thing or the other." With Klimt and Mahler, it was both.

(1986)

6 · *The Composer as Emigrant*

Korngold and Weill, Hollywood and Broadway

A short list of the artists and intellectuals chased West to America by Hitler includes such luminaries as Bertold Brecht, Albert Einstein, Walter Gropius, George Grosz, Thomas Mann, Erwin Piscator, Laszlo Moholy-Nagy, Paul Tillich. One result was an American intellectual community of unprecedented size and force, making the United States, in Virgil Thomson's words, "for the first time an international center for intellectuals," even, as Richard Hofstadter was to put it, "the intellectual capital of the Western world." At the same time, the diversity of this community, its sudden creation and haphazard mixture of native and foreign elements, created stresses within it, and within the culture at large.

The spectacular influx of refugee musicians, together with their complex New World destinies, suggests a microcosm of this larger process of enrichment and assimilation, diversity and strain. The immigrant performers included Adolf Busch, Otto Klemperer, Wanda Landowska, Artur Schnabel, Joseph Szigeti, Bruno Walter. Even more remarkable were the arriving composers; from Germany and Austria alone came Hanns Eisler, Paul Hindemith, Erich Korngold, Ernst Krenek, Arnold Schoenberg, Kurt Weill. With the conspicuous exception of Eisler, who was deported for his political views in 1948, the composers found a haven in the

United States—as well as varying degrees of professional fulfillment.

Some of the factors influencing their adaptability had been startlingly irrelevant before. How old were they? Did they speak English? Was their music already known in the United States? Were they temperamentally suited to courting benefactors and influential friends? Not least important: would their creative personalities mesh with American mores and tastes?

The American setting was tricky. In the years after World War I, America's compositional talents—Samuel Barber, Marc Blitzstein, Aaron Copland, Roy Harris, Walter Piston, Roger Sessions, Virgil Thomson—had returned home in force. Their Old World studies, usually in France, had signified no defection; rather, as Lewis Mumford remarked of Henry James, "absorbtion in Europe [was] a necessary stage in our common development."

And yet the American composer had no certain niche. Grown bigger, more democratic, less cultivated, the American audience increasingly gravitated toward Beethoven and other dead European masters. It was actually tutored—by the "music appreciators" of the 1930s and 1940s—to reject new and native works. Even Copland, who purposely befriended the new audience with works like *Rodeo, Billy the Kid,* and *El salon méxico,* was moved to exclaim:

> Very often I get the impression that audiences seem to think that the endless repetition of a small body of entrenched masterworks is all that is required for a ripe musical culture. . . . Needless to say, I have no quarrel with masterpieces. . . . But when they are used, unwittingly perhaps, to stifle contemporary effort in our country, then I am almost tempted to take the most extreme view and say that we should be better off without them!

These circumstances guaranteed a problematic reception for even the most celebrated emigrant composers. The new audience was predisposed to reject contemporary music. Postwar American composers, intent on fostering a new "American" tradition, were welcoming but wary.

In maximum contrast, the Berlin of Weill and Klemperer, Brecht and Piscator was reckless, experimental, obsessed with modernism. With its forty theaters, 120 newspapers, and four opera houses, Weimar Berlin was a magnet for composers and actors, painters and writers with the urge to do something different and important. Bruno Walter later remembered:

> The common denominator, the characteristic sign of those days, was an unparalleled mental alertness. And the alertness of the giving corresponded to the alertness of the receiving. A passionate general concentration upon cultural life prevailed, eloquently expressed by the large space devoted to art by the daily newspapers in spite of the political excitement of the times.

Berlin vigorously fostered new tendencies of every kind: Dada and *Neue Sachlichkeit, Gebrauchsmusik* and *Zeitoper.* Schoenberg, who would seem such a wild man in the United States, in Berlin seemed already a traditionalist, an elitist, an out-of-touch graybeard consumed by his own importance. Krenek's "jazz opera" *Jonny spielt auf* was the rage, then Weill's *Die Dreigroschenoper,* whose raucous yet sophisticated send-up of high culture was as familiar to Berlin as it was alien to America.

The move to America particularly penalized the novelists and actors, who wrote or spoke English with a foreign accent. For musicians, whose language was "universal," transplantation was less implausible, yet remained tough. Any survey of the performers and composers who relocated to the United States during the 1930s and early 1940s will generally show that even the most eminent had been more widely esteemed and influential in their lands of origin. The great exception was Arturo Toscanini, who became a cult figure in America and yet more bolstered than conteracted American insularity. Toscanini's indifference to new and American music, his preoccupation with executant polish and proficiency, resonated with American prejudices.

The vast majority of the émigrés enjoyed no such adaptation. Of this group, Hindemith and Schoenberg remained famous and productive, yet without looming nearly as large as they had in Germany. Others—Karl Weigl, Alexander von Zemlinsky— loomed so small as to disappear.

As the New World yielded a gamut of outcomes for individual creativity, it also yielded a gamut of informative commentaries by the disgruntled or grateful creators. Schoenberg, at one extreme, found "everything all wrong" in Los Angeles, whose residents could be "kind of helpful" yet were "mostly inferior." In 1946 he wrote to Oskar Kokoschka in New York:

> You complain of lack of culture in this amusement-arcade world [of America]. I wonder what you'd say to the world in which I nearly die of disgust. I don't only mean the "movies." Here is an advertisement by way of example: There's a picture of a man who has run over a child, which is lying dead in front of his car. He clutches his head in despair, but not to say anything like: "My God, what have I done?" For there is a caption saying: "Sorry, now it is too late to worry—take out your policy at the XX Insurance Company in time." And these are the people I'm supposed to teach composition to!

Ernst Krenek was another uncomfortable American. In his view, both he and Schoenberg, and perhaps Bartók, were here discouraged from pursuing "progressive" creative possibilities. Hindemith, he believed, had already sold out before leaving Europe. And Weill had cultivated a new, more mundane American style against his "better judgment."

This certainly was not Weill's opinion. Temperamentally, he was as sanguine as Schoenberg was irascible and extreme. He arrived in America fired with enthusiasm for popular culture and its best possible future. Schoenberg characteristically decried radio and its "boundless surfeit of music." Equally characteristic was Weill's optimistic (and inaccurate) prediction that radio would positively restructure musical life; he anticipated new instruments and composing techniques tailored to broadcasting, and a new, less elitist, less ostentatious concert public. Schoenberg, a hermetic creator, wrote: "If immigration has changed me, I am unaware of it." Weill, who always composed for an audience, felt inspired by America: its democracy, its informality, its decency. Neither of these strategies was "correct"; both worked in personally necessary ways.

A young country, the United States minimized history and tradition. For émigré creators, the outcome could be stultifying or liberating. In fact, America had long been the land of promise and disappointment, hope and frustration. For every Busoni, who marveled in Los Angeles "that *such* a town, so tasteless and bare, could be built in *such* a country," there was a Tchaikovsky, who wrote: "Amazing people these Americans! Compared with Paris . . . the frankness, sincerity, and generosity in this country . . . and its eagerness to please and win approval, are simply astonishing." Anton Rubinstein resented American publicity mongers and autograph hounds, yet called the United States "the land for those who love liberty." Mahler called his New York Philharmonic "a real American orchestra. Untalented and phlegmatic"—and yet he found American audiences "tremendously unspoilt," "more eager to learn and more grateful than any European can imagine." For those who had fled Hitler, and could not turn back, this venerable syndrome of ambivalence was played out with a heightened intensity.

Of the refugee composers, two adapted to the popular arena with particular alacrity: Korngold became Hollywood's most prestigious film composer; Weill succeeded on Broadway. Their destinies, no less than the destinies of those who more painfully

endured the crucible of emigration, illuminated who they were—
and also who we are.

As musical prodigies go, the young Erich Wolfgang Korngold
easily bears comparison with the young Wolfgang Mozart. When
as a nine-year-old, in 1907, he played his cantata *Gold* for Gustav
Mahler, Mahler called him a genius. Four years later, Korngold's
Trio, op. 1, was premiered by an ensemble in which the pianist
was Bruno Walter. Felix Weingartner wrote: "It seems as if nature
has amassed all her gifts into the cradle of this extraordinary
child." His Piano Sonata in E, composed in 1909, was performed
throughout Europe by Artur Schnabel. His ballet-pantomime *Der
Schneeman* was a sensation of the 1910 season at the Vienna Opera.
His *Schauspiel* Overture of 1911 was premiered by Arthur Nikisch
and the Leipzig Gewandhaus Orchestra; this work, and the four-
movement Sinfonietta for large orchestra of 1912, caused Richard
Strauss to exclaim: "Such mastery fills me with awe and fear."
Korngold was now fifteen years old. His first operas, *Der Ring des
Polykrates* and *Violanta,* were given in Munich under Bruno Walter. His String Sextet, op. 10, was widely heard. But his great
international success was the opera *Die tote Stadt,* composed in
1920; it was the vehicle for Maria Jeritza's American debut at the
Metropolitan Opera in 1921. A 1928 poll undertaken by a Viennese newspaper named Korngold and Schoenberg the two greatest
living composers.

Though, like Strauss, Korngold was initially hailed or condemned as a modernist, he proved, like Strauss, to be a diehard
Romantic. His music was, and remained, sensuously chromatic,
rapturously melodic. He did not hide his fondness for operetta,
for confectionary tenderness and splendor. As he also happened
to be the son of Vienna's most feared music critic, the arch-
conservative Julius Korngold, his success was doubly resented by
such progressives as Schoenberg and Webern. Antipathy toward
Korngold's *Das Wunder der Heliane* (1927) was inflamed by feud-

ing between Julius Korngold and supporters of Krenek's *Jonny spielt auf.* (According to Krenek, in a 1990 interview: "Julius Korngold was an enemy of mine. He was very conservative. His main interest was in his son.")

Given his conservatism and facility, Korngold was obviously better equipped to adapt to American audiences than fellow Austrian refugees such as Schoenberg and Krenek. In fact, his adaptation preceded his exile. In the 1920s he had begun accepting commissions to revise operettas for revival—assignments he handled with typical fluency and flair. In 1929 he collaborated with Max Reinhardt on a new version of *Die Fledermaus,* including interpolations from other Johann Strauss scores. When Reinhardt went to Hollywood in 1934 to direct Mickey Rooney, Olivia de Havilland, and James Cagney in *A Midsummer Night's Dream,* he took Korngold with him to supervise the application of Mendelssohn's incidental music. Korngold created new numbers by borrowing from Mendelssohn's *Scottish* and *Italian* symphonies and *Songs without Words.* He ingeniously underscored the dialogue in places by conducting the tempos and rhythms of the actors' spoken delivery, then, using headphones, adding the corresponding music weeks later.

Warner Brothers was impressed and offered him a contract. Korngold signed after securing privileges no other studio composer enjoyed. He would be permitted to score as few as two films a year. He could return to Vienna at least six months out of every twelve. And he was free to re-use his film music as he saw fit. Korngold's subsequent scores for *Captain Blood* and *Anthony Adverse* made him America's leading composer of symphonic film music. When Hitler occupied Austria in 1938, Korngold (who was Jewish) settled in the United States together with his wife, sons, and father.

All told, Korngold scored nineteen Hollywood films between 1935 and 1954, including *The Prince and the Pauper, The Adventures of Robin Hood, The Sea Hawk,* and *King's Row* (with Ronald Reagan's most-admired performance). With his *King's Row* score, Korngold joined company with the many foreign-born producers, directors, and writers who helped define Hollywood's version of America. (The fanfare-like *King's Row* theme—the best-known music Korngold wrote for the movies—was played at both Reagan inaugurations.) His nine-to-five colleagues sometimes began a new film the morning after finishing the one before; Korngold, averaging one film a year, was a pampered star. He received prominent billing and won two Academy Awards.

Korngold took Hollywood seriously. He assumed that movie audiences were no more or less sophisticated than concert audiences. In 1940 he wrote:

> When, in the projection room or through the operator's little window, I am watching the picture unroll, when I am sitting at the piano improvising or inventing themes and tunes, when I am facing the orchestra conducting my music, I have the feeling that I am giving my own and my best: symphonically dramatic music which fits the picture, its action and its psychology, and which, nevertheless, will be able to hold its own in the concert hall. . . . Never have I differentiated between music for films and that for the operas and concert pieces.

And these claims hold true. With their leitmotifs and thematic development, Korngold's film scores really do resemble—as he once put it—"operas without singing." In terms of style, sound, and purpose, they represent a scant departure from his 1919 incidental music for *Much Ado about Nothing*. Hollywood, moreover, had since the 1920s welcomed highbrow musical accompaniments. Of the early talkies, *King Kong* (1933), with a seventy-five-minute score by the Viennese Max Steiner, proved a landmark in legitimizing lush symphonic soundtracks supporting dialogue as well as action. Compared to Britain, France, or Germany, America showed little interest in soliciting film music from its important contemporary composers; the studios preferred comfortably old-fashioned—and hence European—sonic upholstery. But this did not preclude individuality. No Hollywood composer was more individual—or, even in Sherwood Forest, more Viennese—than Korngold. Christopher Palmer, in his *The Composer in Hollywood* (1990), writes that Korngold "arrived in Hollywood at precisely the right moment, since film music was still struggling to find its feet, and [he] brought it a sorely needed dignity, stature, and professionalism. He was excited by the medium and unstintingly gave his best."

To a degree both surprising and enlightening, Hollywood adapted to Korngold, not the other way round.

Korngold vowed not to compose again for the concert hall until "that monster in Europe is removed from the world." With the end of World War II, he mainly turned his back on Hollywood and resumed writing absolute music.

Bronislaw Huberman had urged Korngold to compose a violin concerto. Yet it was not Huberman but Jascha Heifetz who premiered Korngold's 1945 Concerto in D with the Saint Louis Symphony, conducted by Vladimir Golschmann, on February 15, 1947. The excited Saint Louis reception—one critic predicted that Korngold's concerto would endure as long as Mendelssohn's—was encouraging. Korngold now composed, among other works, a Cello Concerto, a Serenade for Strings, and a song cycle. His swan song was the hour-long Symphony in F-sharp, finished in 1952. This music was not altogether neglected. Heifetz performed the Violin Concerto in New York, Chicago, and Los Angeles, and recorded it in 1953 with Alfred Wallenstein and the Los Angeles Philharmonic. In Europe, Otto Klemperer conducted it, with Bronislaw Gimpel as soloist. Wilhelm Furtwängler gave the first performance of the Serenade. But Korngold could not find a conductor willing to undertake his symphony. When he returned to Vienna in 1949, hoping to resume his professional life where it had left off eleven years earlier, he found himself written off as a Hollywood anomaly, a has-been, an anachronism.

And, in fact, Korngold did seem untouched by the violent cultural and political currents of the previous decades. Perhaps he was temperamentally immune to modernism and its wrenching sociopolitical backdrop (the violinist Felix Galimir, who knew Korngold in Vienna in the thirties, remembers him as "child-like, very simple and unaffected"). Perhaps California had insulated Korngold, had cut him off from his cultural inheritance and truncated his creative potential. Or perhaps Hollywood's fantasy world of princes and pirate kings supplied evasions that Korngold, lost in the past, subconsciously craved.

In any event, he emerged from his Hollywood hibernation as from a time warp. Just as he had once borrowed Robin Hood's theme from the 1921 symphonic overture *Sursum Corda,* Korngold now borrowed from four film scores in composing his Violin Concerto. This infiltration in no sense implies a pastiche; rather, it confirms the essential unity of Korngold's screen and concert styles.

The high cultural climate of the 1950s and 1960s, in which "serious" contemporary music was typically esoteric, made Korngold—whether of Hollywood or Vienna—anathema to sophisticates. Today, with intellectuals slumming in pop culture and questioning the political premises of modernism, we are much less prone to hierarchize "high" versus "low." And so we recall Korngold with new interest and fewer (or different) prejudices. *Die tote Stadt* has been revived in Vienna (1967), in New York (1975), in Berlin (1983), and also recorded under Erich Leinsdorf (1976). The Symphony in F-sharp was belatedly premiered in Munich by Rudolf Kempe (1972), who subsequently recorded it (1974). Ulf Hoelscher and Itzhak Perlman, among others, have recorded the Violin Concerto (1974, 1977). The film scores have been newly recorded and acclaimed.

To Brendan G. Carroll, president of the Erich Wolfgang Korngold Society and author of a Korngold biography-in-the-making, Korngold belongs to a rediscovered "late Romantic German school" also including Franz Schmidt, Franz Schreker, and Alexander von Zemlinsky, and the Korngold saga is "the story of an extraordinary composer who, because of the caprices of political history and musical fashion, became the victim of unjust neglect." Other rediscoverers of Korngold may decide that, landing in Hollywood, he fortuitously located his ideal metier, protected from the challenge of deeper creative aspirations he could not fathom. If so, his adaptation differed fundamentally from that of another refugee who refashioned his music for America's cultural marketplace: Kurt Weill.

"Opera will be one of the essential factors in that universally apparent development which is heralding the coming liquidation of all the bourgeois arts," wrote Kurt Weill in a 1927 essay, "Zeitoper," calling for opera composers to address a "wider," more "naive" audience. Bertolt Brecht, meanwhile, played, sang, and absorbed music in the cabarets and bars of Munich and Berlin. According to his biographer Martin Esslin: "He hated Beethoven and the sound of violins, but liked Bach and Mozart. But above all he disliked the atmosphere of concerts: the spectacle of frock-coated gentlemen sawing away at their instruments, of polite and educated people gently bored and pretending to be moved."

Artists and intellectuals of Weimar Germany resolved to smash distinctions between popular and high culture. Rejecting the passionate subjectivity of the Romantics and their expressionist progeny, they championed cultural democracy and *Neue Sachlichkeit* ("new objectivity"), the latter a matter-of-fact aesthetic stressing practicality and self-discipline. Paul Hindemith—experimenting with jazz and film, moving toward a pragmatic, nonelitist *Gebrauchsmusik* ("music for use")—was one representative *neue sachlicher* composer; in France, Milhaud and Stravinsky, while less political, likewise gravitated toward lowbrow musical sources.

This was the climate in which Weill and Brecht converged. Their fitful partnership began with the *Mahagonny Songspiel*

(1927), commissioned by Hindemith's Deutsche Kammermusik Baden-Baden. As Weill was ultimately more oriented toward a type of humane, socially relevant opera, and Brecht more interested in a combative theater-with-songs, they eventually parted ways. But their short collaboration was historic; it also produced, among other works, *Aufstieg und Fall der Stadt Mahagonny* (1929); *Happy End* (1929); the school opera *Der Jasager* (1930); *Die sieben Todsünden* (1933); and their signature creation: *Die Dreigroschenoper* (*The Threepenny Opera*) of 1928.

It may have been Brecht's English-speaking secretary Elisabeth Hauptmann who suggested that he rework John Gay's *The Beggar's Opera*. First produced in London in 1728, it had been successfully revived there in 1920. With its scheming thieves and whores, its provocative intermingling of quotidian and "serious," its send-up of Handelian conventions, Gay's "ballad opera" suited the themes and temper of Weimar culture. Brecht set out to adapt *The Beggar's Opera* as "an opera for beggars . . . cheap enough for beggars to be able to watch": a "Threepenny Opera." The insidious biblical allusions of his *Dreigroschenoper* libretto, its tart epigrams and wicked rhymes, constitute a study in irreverence. Weill's music, too, makes a meal of mockery, feeding on opera, on operetta, on Romantic largesse.

Die Dreigroschenoper received its premiere on August 31, 1928, at Berlin's Theater an Schiffbauerdamm. The house was nearly empty; the producer, Ernst Josef Aufricht, expected the show to close after—if not actually during—the first night. But the "Kanonen-Song" brought the puzzled audience to life. Aufricht later recalled: "Clapping, shouting, stamping their feet, they demanded an encore. . . . From this moment on, every line, every note, was a success." The production ran for 250 consecutive performances, after which it moved to another theater. Count Harry Kessler wrote in his diary: "It's all the rage, permanently sold out. We bumped into the Prittwitzens (the ambassador and wife), the Herbert Guttmanns (member of the board of the Dresdner Bank and his wife), etc. One simply has to have been there."

But Brecht had intended a consciousness-raising polemic. In a 1933 interview with himself, he mused:

> *What, in your opinion, accounted for the success of Die Drei-groschenoper?*
> I'm afraid it was everything that didn't matter to me: the romantic plot, the love story, the music. . . .
> *And what would have mattered to you?*
> The critique of society.

One key to the show's acclaim was 1920s Berlin itself. "All values were changed, and not only material ones," observed Stefan Zweig.

> The laws of the State were flouted, no tradition, no moral code was respected, Berlin was transformed into the Babylon of the world. Bars, amusement parks, honky-tonks sprang up like mushrooms. . . . Along the entire Kurfurstendamm powdered and rouged young men sauntered, and they were not all professionals; every high-school boy wanted to earn some money and in the dimly lit bars one might see government officials and men of the world of finance tenderly courting drunken sailors without any shame. Even the Rome of Suetonius had never known such orgies as the pervert balls of Berlin, where hundreds of men costumed as women and hundreds of women as men danced under the benevolent eyes of the police.

Elias Canetti, a Berlin resident at the time, observed of *Die Dreigroschenoper* in his memoirs:

> It was the most precise expression of Berlin. The people cheered themselves, they saw themselves, and were pleased. . . . Now it had been said, no bug in a rug could have felt snugger. . . . Only those who experienced it can

believe the grating and bare self-satisfaction that ema-
nated from this production ... everything was glorified
that one would otherwise shamefully conceal. Most fit-
tingly and effectively derided was sympathy.

But moralists of the extreme right condemned Brecht as a
Marxist, Weill as a Jew. It was the Nazis, not the fashionably dis-
solute bourgeoisie, who understood *Die Dreigroschenoper* as Brecht
had intended: a mockery of "respectable" music and theater; a
withering assault on capitalism. A week after Hitler seized power
in early 1933, a new production of *Die Dreigroschenoper* opened in
Hildesheim. The Weill scholar Stephen Hinton conjectures this
was the last production of the work in Germany until August
1945. At the 1938 Düsseldorf exhibit of *Entartete Musik* (degener-
ate music), an entire room was devoted to *Die Dreigroschenoper*—
only to attract such appreciative crowds that it apparently had to
be closed.

Weill left Berlin for Paris in 1933. Though he was Germany's
most successful stage composer, his success was by no means international; in France, his prospects proved ambiguous. He first came
to the United States in 1935 and took steps toward acquiring
American citizenship two years later. By then, America had become home. He died in New York in 1950, only fifty years old.

The America Weill discovered in 1935 was a world removed
from Weimar politics, Weimar culture, Weimar audiences. The
United States premiere of *The Threepenny Opera,* two years before,
had failed dismally; Manhattan's critics had found it dreary and
perplexing. During his remaining fifteen years, not one of the
stage works Weill completed in Europe was professionally
mounted in the United States. When he died, the assessor of his
estate declared *Die Dreigroschenoper* "worthless," of "no salable
value."

But Weill, who quickly mastered English following his arrival
in the New World, had been determined to adapt and to leave
Die Dreigroschenoper behind. He surrounded himself with the best

American dramatists he could find. For Broadway—he had no use for opera—he turned out a string of box office hits, including *Lady in the Dark* (with Moss Hart and Ira Gershwin) and *One Touch of Venus* (with S. J. Perelman and Ogden Nash). Though he dreamed of mediating between opera and Broadway, he had essentially transformed himself into a more popular composer than he had ever been in Europe. And yet Weill's fervent populism was such that he made the transition eagerly. Alienating old admirers, he acquired followers who knew nothing of his previous career.

More recently, interest in all phases of Weill's catalog, and in Weill the man, has as much sustained as resolved controversy over his American transformation. Of the many reconsiderations and summings-up, none is more provocative than David Drew's, in the *New Grove Dictionary of Music and Musicians:*

> Whatever one may think of the creative results, it is clear that Weill's Broadway achievements called for at least as much human courage and determination as any of his earlier ones, and perhaps more. It is equally clear that they exacted from him a degree of self-sacrifice greater than any that would have been demanded by a totalitarian ministry of culture. The difference between Weill up to 1934 and Weill after 1940 is not attributable to any development which could be described as normal, or even as clinically predictable. While some notable artists have simply stopped creating at a certain stage in their careers and a few have put an end to their lives, Weill is perhaps the only one to have done away with his old creative self in order to make way for a new one.

The irony of Korngold's adaptation to America is that it was no adaptation at all. The irony of Weill's adaptation is that it was eclipsed by something he had left behind: his greatest and most enduring American success was not *One Touch of Venus,* or *Lady in the Dark,* or any of five other pieces composed for the American stage. *The Threepenny Opera,* revived off-Broadway in 1954 in Marc Blitzstein's translation, played for 2,611 consecutive performances, surpassing *Oklahoma!* as the longest-running musical in the history of the American theater until that time. In Berlin, *Die Dreigroschenoper* succeeded because it mirrored a decadence that Berliners fondly recognized. In America, *Threepenny Opera* succeeded because its decadence proved an exotic diversion. Four years into its fabulous off-Broadway run, the producers remarked: "Neither of us did [*Threepenny Opera*] because we liked Brecht's social criticism. We did it because we thought it was a great show."

(1991)

7 · *The World's Greatest Piano Career*

The Transformations of Vladimir Horowitz

The 1991 posthumous release of *Horowitz: The Last Recording* completed this century's greatest piano career. Vladimir Horowitz's final recording, dating from October and November 1989, when the pianist was eighty-six years old, radiates wisdom. Ideally, it would consummate an evolutionary arc, a rounded span of accumulated ripeness. But the Horowitz career was dramatically fitful, never smooth. And his *Last Recording* documents no consummation, but the final twist in a success story contorted by ironies, a portrait of the famous artist as a casualty of circumstances beyond his control.

Horowitz never had to court fame in the United States; it courted him. His explosive American debut, playing Tchaikovsky with the New York Philharmonic on January 12, 1928, raised the roof. Upon settling in the United States in 1939 at the age of thirty-six, he became known as the quintessential Romantic virtuoso. With Arturo Toscanini and Jascha Heifetz, he topped RCA Victor's pantheon of world greats; it was as a proprietary article of faith that Americans proclaimed him the leading pianist of his time. In a later phase, signaled by a new record label (Deutsche Grammophon), the Horowitz career found ever new outlets for exposure and publicity. Nineteen eighty-five was the year of his first film, *Vladimir Horowitz: The Last Romantic.* In 1986 he returned to Russia—the occasion for a television special, a best-selling, Grammy Award–winning recording, and a *Time* cover story. Then, a year later, DG offered *Horowitz Plays Mozart,* the dividends being another film, another best-selling recording, and another Grammy.

Horowitz moved from DG to Sony Classical in October 1989—just in time for his *Last Recording.* The repertoire proved uncannily correct: two of Chopin's late, valedictory nocturnes, a sublime Romantic leave-taking; Liszt's variations on Bach's "Weinen, Klagen, Sorgen, Zagen," a purgative lament; Liszt's transcription of the *Liebestod* from Wagner's *Tristan und Isolde.* These works and five others were recorded during six sessions over a period of thirteen days. The *Liebestod,* an afterthought, was the last music Horowitz touched at the sixth session, on Wednesday, November 1. A final session was planned for the following Friday, but Horowitz had an upset stomach and had to cancel. He died suddenly three days later. When Thomas Frost, Horowitz's record producer since 1985, listened to the tapes, he discovered that the missing final session had been unnecessary. Frost later wrote: "For the last few years, Horowitz had been recording at the leisurely pace of two sessions per week, and since he rarely worked more than two hours per session, we needed about three weeks to complete a recording. This time, however, Horowitz was driven by some mysterious source of energy."

In fact, Horowitz was from the start a merchandiser's dream. Even his notorious unreliability was turned to his advantage. No film star played such tantalizing games of hide-and-seek. He retired at least three times: 1936–38, 1953–65, and 1969–74. When he died, he had not played in public for more than two years. There had been talk of a couple of recitals in Europe in mid-December.

Had Horowitz's withdrawals seemed ploys, they would merely have irritated. Instead, they seemed necessities. No other musician projected such electrifying insecurity. Horowitz exerted the fascination of a psychological and physical mechanism strung so taut that it had to careen out of control yet did not—usually. No wonder his disappearances bred rumors of shock therapy and institutionalization. Then, each time he remastered his will to perform, curiosity ran riot. Were the legendary fingers still as accurate and fast? Could the legendary sonorities still shake the stage? And also, more revealingly: Had Horowitz the musician ripened with age? Could he silence nagging doubts that the world's greatest pianist was not a great artist? To reassure us, his advocates periodically proclaimed a "new Horowitz."

Was Horowitz a great artist? At first American critics answered "no." "Too uncomfortably brilliant," reported William Spier in *Musical America.* "His fingers allow him no repose. They are still in the puppy stage." In the opinion of the *Nation,* Horowitz reduced "every emotion to black and white, and every intention to technique." "The prevailing impression that he left was of power and rapidity," wrote Pitts Sanborn in the *Evening Telegram.* "Rarely, if ever, have I heard a piano so unashamedly banged." There was no question of the breathtaking élan, intensity, and virtuosity of Horowitz the instrumentalist—of his "magnificent muscularity," "heaven-storming octaves," "phenomenal strength and speed," and "fine control of dynamics." To most New York critics, the twenty-five-year-old Russian expatriate seemed a pianist of fabulous promise. For the New York public, he was already fabulous.

But Horowitz's critics soon caught up with his adoring public. Just as America's concert audiences grew suddenly larger during the music appreciation decades of the 1930s and 1940s, a new breed of music critic took over. Before World War I—before the radio and the phonograph, before proliferating orchestras and eager pedagogues—the leading reviewers had been armchair aesthetes like the *New York Tribune*'s Henry Krehbiel. The next generation of critics mounted soapboxes and grabbed shirtsleeves. These ebullient populists were as trusting of public opinion as the old guard had been circumspect. And many of them were less worldly; disdaining an Old World polarized and "fatigued" by the

Great War, they bragged of a superior (yet imported) New World concert culture.

Olin Downes, who joined the *New York Times* in 1924, became the model mainstream music critic; he identified with *vox populi,* and even aspired to disappear into it. Other leading populists included Howard Taubman, also of the *Times* music staff, and Samuel Chotzinoff of the *New York Post.* These critics, and others like them, joined in the cheering for Horowitz. All three were also Toscanini fans. Like Horowitz, Toscanini had aroused unrestrained American popular acclaim first, unrestrained critical acclaim second. When, in 1933, Horowitz married Toscanini's younger daughter, Wanda, Horowitz (who now placed his father-in-law's photograph on his piano) began to acquire something like Toscanini's aura of integrity. Their joint celebrity was mutually validating.

Then Horowitz's first, 1936 retirement intervened, setting the stage for his first comeback and the first "new" Horowitz. According to 1939 press releases, Horowitz had vastly matured. He collected fine art and read fine books. His collaborations with Toscanini, in concertos by Brahms and Tchaikovsky, ostensibly measured commensurate artistic gains. "Nothing Mr. Horowitz has done here has indicated more impressively his growth as interpreter as well as virtuoso of his instrument," wrote Olin Downes of a Horowitz-Toscanini Brahms Second Concerto in 1940. When, eight years later, Horowitz and Toscanini played the Brahms B-flat again, *Time* discerned "new maturity and depth." But it was Taubman who played the Horowitz-equals-Toscanini equation to the hilt. "The wild, volatile virtuoso of two years ago has become one of the most mature, responsible musicians," wrote Taubman in 1948. And now Horowitz was also a mature, responsible man.

> He is slim and well groomed, and he looks more like a man of affairs than the conventional figure of the musician. . . . There are paintings on the walls [of Horowitz's

studio] by Manet, Pissarro, Renoir and Degas; there are good books, and with Horowitz and his wife there is good talk, not only about music but about politics, economics, psychology, what you will.

. . . Like his father-in-law, he does not like formal interviews. . . . Like his father-in-law, he has a charming simplicity.

Five years later, Taubman declared "The Transformation of Vladimir Horowitz": "Away from the piano and the concert hall he seems to have arrived at a greater inner relaxation than he used to have, and that in turn stems from the things that have been happening to him as a musician. . . . 'We have matured together, the public and I,' he says." And there were further Toscanini analogies: like his father-in-law, whom he resembled "in many ways," Horowitz had turned down huge fees for "unworthy" projects; like his father-in-law, he aimed "to make every phrase sing."

In fact, Horowitz and the indomitable Toscanini were remarkably unlike one another, as musicians and men; and neither was the regular guy Americans like Taubman made him out to be. As for Horowitz's new inner relaxation: two months following his announced "transformation," he quit the stage, a victim of nervous collapse. And yet, incredibly, the new Horowitz endured. Chotzinoff wrote in 1964:

Horowitz has read and studied extraordinarily much during his "sabbatical." . . . [He has] arrived at interpretive conclusions that represent a new phase in his relation to his art, and not alone in music for the piano. He has arrived at a point which very few virtuoso performers ever achieve, or want to achieve. He has, through study and contemplation, come to believe in the absolute supremacy of the composer, the same belief that is the foundation of the art of his great father-in-law.

Reviewing Horowitz's dramatic 1965 comeback, Harold Schonberg in the *Times* heard "a grander, more spacious line," and interpretations "emotionally more poised, more of a piece, less driving and nervous." Then, two decades later, came the poise and maturity of Horowitz in Mozart. Though he had never been associated with this composer, he now called Mozart "number one." According to an essay accompanying DG's *Horowitz Plays Mozart,* "Horowitz has loved the music of Mozart all his life, and one of his favorite pastimes is reading the composer's letters." For new Horowitz purposes, Mozart became the latest, truest validator of ripeness. Horowitz would shed Romantic excess, recapture innocence, lay bare his soul. But this was not to be.

Horowitz's recordings shed perspective on his singular career. The best known of the early ones, made in London not so long after he left Russia in 1925, are of the Rachmaninoff Third Concerto (1930) and the Liszt B minor Sonata (1932). Both performances are plainer and more direct than his later style. The Liszt is memorable partly for the pianist's distinctness of articulation at phenomenal speeds—a feat epitomized by passages of decorative filigree as prickly as a comb being stroked along its teeth. The demonism is real, yet purely instrumental: young Horowitz skims Liszt's Faustian striving and religious rapture. In the simpler "Gretchen" music, his fingers take on a restless, irrelevant life of their own.

After moving to New York in 1939 and basing his career in the United States (between 1951 and 1982 he was never heard in Europe), Horowitz rerecorded both works for RCA Victor: the Liszt Sonata in 1976, the Rachmaninoff Concerto in 1951 and again in 1978. The complex, layered surfaces of these readings document Horowitz's application of ever more elaborate voicings and rubatos. The two performances from the 1970s are brutal, labored affairs. Already, in the 1951 Rachmaninoff, Horowitz's lunging accents and surprise dynamics reflect a *coup de théâtre* mentality. Obviously, this reading is tremendous in its way. The climaxes throb with Horowitz's trademark combination of easy power and convulsive intensity. But it was the young Van Cliburn, recording Rachmaninoff's Third in concert a month after winning the 1958 Tchaikovsky competition, who made it sound memorably beautiful.

Could there possibly have been a period when this "world's greatest pianist" excelled in important music? One of his most sophisticated, most admired recorded performances is a 1969 version of *Kreisleriana*. The playing is tasteful, unmistakably poised. Horowitz's impulsive spontaneity, his wondrous ten-voice range of touch, color, and dynamics, suits Schumann's Romantic abandon. *Kreisleriana*'s inspirational sources include E. T. A. Hoffmann's witty and eccentric Kapellmeister Kreisler, and Clara Wieck, Schumann's loving wife-to-be. To my hearing, these components of *Kreisleriana* mainly elude Horowitz. Schumann's third *Kreisleriana* fantasy is a portrait in teasing grotesquerie, its central motif being a limping four-note figure distorted by its odd second member.

In Horowitz's performance, the second note is swallowed, smoothing the triplet into two sixteenth notes and canceling Schumann's eccentricity. The sixth *Kreisleriana* fantasy contains some of Schumann's tenderest pages. But Horowitz's interpretation sounds activated by tactile sensation: dramatizing the indicated accents and dynamic shifts, he disrupts the interiority of tone. Schumann's shy, confiding intimacy—his lover's whisper—is silenced. One is mainly aware of Horowitz, the pianist. For all the inner voices he extracts, he misses Schumann's inner voice.

Scriabin is probably the important composer Horowitz served most completely. As in Rachmaninoff, the intricate textures keep the fingers busy; more than in Rachmaninoff, the nervous currents build to manic climaxes. Horowitz came surprisingly late to his Scriabin repertoire, acquiring it mainly in the 1950s and 1960s. In the United States, which also came late to Scriabin, Horowitz seemed Scriabin's prophet; Harold Schonberg bolstered conventional wisdom when he wrote in the *Times* in 1965, "Nobody plays Scriabin better than Mr. Horowitz. [He possesses] complete affinity with [this] strange, mysterious world." In Russia, meanwhile, the dominant Scriabin interpreter was the composer's son-in-law, Vladimir Sofronitzki (1902–63). A 1960 recording of Sofronitzky in concert documents the pianist in a trance, playing twenty-six Scriabin selections without interruption, one flowing into the next in a gathering, obsessive tide capped by the frenzied trills and hallucinatory night lights of the Ninth Sonata (the *Black Mass*). By this standard, Horowitz's Scriabin, however mesmerizing, seems as far from Scriabin's actual mysticism as his B minor Sonata is from Lisztian exaltation.

In fact, Horowitz typically excelled in lesser music: brains-in-the-fingers cameos by minor Romantics. At his famous 1965 comeback recital at Carnegie Hall, the crowd saved its loudest roar for a ninety-second encore: Horowitz's performance of Moszkowski's Etude in A-flat major, op. 72, no. 11 (preserved on the in-concert recording) is not just an astounding lesson in high-speed articulation; it is equally a lesson in interpretation. The lightning swells and diminuendos, the sudden dabs of color, the vanishing-act coda, whose four floating chords ascend into silence—these and other sleights-of-hand prove magically self-sufficient. And Horowitz retained such magic powers into his eighties. The best of his 1985 studio recordings is of Karl Tausig's technicolor transcription of Schubert's *Marche militaire*, D. 733, no. 1. Horowitz sounds happiest, most completely himself, in this type of music. Employing his clairvoyant aural imagination, his prankster's sense of fun, he empties his full bag of tricks. Depth, decorum, fidelity are unnecessary, even out of place; a superior sort of pandering is the very *raison d'être*. Applied to unadulterated Schubert on the same recording, the Horowitz treatment sounds fussy but plausible; the B-flat Impromptu is itself a divertissement, sublimated Viennese *Hausmusik*. It is in Mozart's Sonata in B-flat, K. 333, recorded two years later, that Horowitz's aversion to simplicity proves fatal.

In conjunction with Mozart's economy—every note tells—Horowitz's restless detailing ensures an informational overload. Conditioned by a lifetime of playing to the galleries, he exaggerates every nuance. His inflated rubatos and delayed downbeats gum the line. His pedaled half-tints are not sweet but cleverly saccharine. Quoted in an album note, Horowitz argues that Mozart "was really a Romantic composer," even "a virtuoso-composer just like Chopin or Liszt." But the problem with Horowitz's Mozart is less one of style than of substance. Edwin Fischer, Wilhelm Kempff, Clifford Curzon played Mozart as colorfully as Horowitz does. Mieczyslaw Horszowski, in a 1986 Nonesuch recording made weeks before his ninety-fourth birthday, offers Mozart playing teeming with ideas; performing the D minor Fantasy (K. 397), he opens himself fearlessly to the experience of innocence.

Could the Horowitz career have evolved differently? Horowitz's early recordings of Liszt and Rachmaninoff are unmannered. A 1934 version of the finale of Tchaikovsky's First Piano Concerto with the Danish Radio Orchestra under Nikolai Malko—the earliest available recording of Horowitz in concert—is elegant: as deft, as lyrically aromatic and airy as his 1943 performance with Toscanini, also recorded in concert, is brutal and blunt. Boris Asafyev, the preeminent Soviet musicologist of his time, once praised a 1923 Horowitz recital for (among other virtues) its "clarity and simplicity of purpose in combination with refined elegance and grace." One can understand why political turmoil impelled Horowitz to leave Russia; at the same time, his musician's role was healthier there: the child of a cultivated family, connected to the musical elite, he composed, he played chamber music and partnered singers (he once accompanied *Winterreise* from memory), his solo repertoire was huge and not unadventurous.*

But Horowitz's move to the United States doomed him to a

---

*It speaks volumes that Horowitz's 1920s sonata partner was the aristocratic Nathan Milstein.

career of maximum fame, fortune, and virtuosic display. The populist fervor of America's new audience, intensified by wartime patriotic fervor, excited possessive adulation of expatriate celebrity
performers—and imposed commensurate expectations on the
performers themselves. RCA's relentless "world's greatest" hype,
the aggressive salesmanship of Columbia Concerts' Arthur Judson
(who at one time had Horowitz playing an average of one concert
every two days), the harsh scrutiny of Toscanini (who, pace Howard Taubman, intimidated his son-in-law)—it would have taken a
saint to resist these influences. Hypersensitive, insecure, Horowitz
was no saint. His playing turned nervous, neurotically intense.
According to his pupil Byron Janis, Horowitz advised him to "do
things simply for the sake of arresting the audience's attention—
a sudden pianissimo, an unexpected accent . . . you must exagger-
ate." On another occasion, Horowitz was quoted confessing, "If
you play Classic music in correct style on a big piano and in a big
hall, it will bore most of the audience."

Of course, not every aspect of Horowitz's career and influence
bore the taint of his devouring celebrity. His fellow pianists were
seduced by his miraculous sound. And they followed his brave
lead when he explored Scriabin, or Scarlatti and Clementi, or
lesser-known works of Chopin and Schumann. To the musical
public at large, however, Horowitz did not—could not—exist
apart from his hyperbolic reputation. Latterly, in the age of Pavarotti, the imagery of personal extravagance deeply inflected the
imagery of "world's greatest pianist." In *Time*'s Horowitz cover
story of May 5, 1986, the "new Horowitz"—his playing in Moscow was "infused with a passionate fire and breathtaking precision
not heard in years"—was "the last romantic, whose artless, effortless, larger-than-life pianism . . . is a vanishing art." Concomitantly, Horowitz's validating signatures included a Romantic,
larger-than-life personality, and larger-than-life fees.

Certainly, Horowitz comports himself with the regal
mien of a 19th century monarch. He performs only on

Sunday afternoons at 4. No matter where he is playing, he dines on Dover or gray sole flown in fresh that day. His wife, his housekeeper, his manager, his piano technician and a Steinway official all accompany him—as does, of course, his piano. The $40,000 concert grand [is] plucked by crane from the living room of his Manhattan townhouse.... In their 14 room white stone townhouse on Manhattan's Upper East Side, purchased in 1947 for $30,000 and now worth a hundred times that amount, the Horowitzes live quietly, comfortably, and just a little eccentrically. They eat out practically every night, chauffeured to one of a few favorite, mostly Italian restaurants, where Horowitz dines on pasta and the inevitable sole. After returning home, he relaxes by watching a triple feature of adventure and horror movies (*The Terminator, Halloween, Raiders of the Lost Ark*) on his videocassette recorder, then turns in about 4 a.m. and sleeps until noon. He no longer smokes, does not drink and never eats meat.

He is one of the highest-paid musicians in the world, commanding a fee of as much as half a million dollars for a single concert and never less than $100,000.

This cartoon, to which Horowitz had to live up (or down), was one cost of playing the celebrity game. Nothing more illuminates Horowitz's artistic fate as a celebrity musician than the 1987 film *Horowitz Plays Mozart.* Recording the A major Piano Concerto, K. 488, with Carlo Maria Giulini and the La Scala Orchestra, Horowitz is mainly attuned to people: players, listeners, technicians, music businessmen. Warming up, he plays a bit of the K. 333 Sonata, turns to the first violins, and offers, "That will be on the other side [of the recording]." His what-do-you-think-of-me expression is answered with bravos and applause. Upon completing the first movement of K. 488, he blows the orchestra a kiss and remarks, "Very good." "That was very beautiful, Maestro," comments Frost, the producer for DG. Certain critics have been invited; during a break, Horowitz wants to know if they find his playing "too free," and he has Frost ask them. The second movement is now recorded. Though it is one of Mozart's raptest reveries, Horowitz eagerly signals to Giulini, smiling and nodding, as soon as he is done playing, before Giulini and the orchestra have finished. He also bounces his importunate smiles and nods off his page turner; at one point, upon flubbing some passagework, he turns to the young man and giggles naughtily, shoulders hunched, hand over mouth. The session completed, he mugs for the camera, then blackens its lens with his hand. In the control room, hearing a playback, he flamboyantly mimes playing and conducting, even listening. "That was better," he comments. "That is good." "Very good." Giulini and Frost cooperate; Horowitz's very face, unhappy in repose, craves a response.

The Horowitz of 1987 was no newer than the new Horowitz who came out of retirement in 1939, or the new Horowitz who played Brahms with Toscanini in 1948, or the new Horowitz who was "transformed" by "greater inner relaxation" in 1953, or the new Horowitz who studied and read on sabbatical in 1964, or the new Horowitz who returned to Carnegie Hall in 1965, or to Moscow in 1986. Even Mozart could not make Horowitz seem new. But perhaps his *Last Recording* can; it lends credence, at last, to the many stories of Horowitz playing differently at home when he was "comfortable" and "relaxed." The interpretations, the pianism, are absolutely undemonstrative. For once, he indulges in no stunts (or only one: a swollen trill at the close of Chopin's E minor Etude, op. 25, no. 5). There is no "performing," no nervous effort to arrest our attention. Addressing a valedictory repertoire, this new, subdued Horowitz actually sounds reflective.

The aroma of death hangs sweetly upon the Wagner-Liszt *Liebestod*. Horowitz's wizard's touch of hand and foot sifts and soothes the polymorphous play of sound. The climax is dispersed. It is a gentle passage to death, a venerable sorcerer's etherealization.

What has happened to the old Horowitz, whose agitation precluded serenity? One new factor is prosaic: a different piano. As on his previous, 1986–89 recording, *Horowitz at Home,* Horowitz has abandoned his signature Steinway, with its hard hammers. The substitute Steinway, an instrument moved into his apartment several years earlier, is warmer and mellower. It sounds like a piano.

And Horowitz's advanced age and reduced firepower could only have weakened his addiction to dynamic and interpretive excess. Still, something more must have changed. Mordecai Shehori, the Israeli-American pianist who turned pages for Horowitz at all his last recording sessions, tells me:

> He was a different person. Much less neurotic. Much more serious, more introspective. And he was very eager to do it—there was no fooling around. At one point, he listened to a playback and said to me: "We cannot use this, it's much too mannered." I do think he had an intimation he was going to die.
>
> You know, any pianist's playing changes according to who you're playing for. If you're sensitive. In Horowitz's case, this sensitivity—to everyone and everything around him—was amazingly acute, as naked as an open wound. He played this game of being goofy and frivolous, but he was very aware both of his gifts and of his faults. Probably, he had a fragile ego—a desperate need to reach people. Invariably, he would watch me listen to his playing; he needed a response. His tragedy was that he was always surrounded by flatterers, who complimented him on everything. But I couldn't do that, and he realized it. I found that, by enthusiastically acknowledging when he played sincerely, with depth of feeling, I was able to encourage him toward greater introversion. I listened to him very intensely when he played like this—so he was satisfied that it wasn't boring.

Some will find this a self-serving statement, but I do not. The film *Horowitz Plays Mozart* makes visible what the ears detect: Horowitz was less immersed in music than he was aware of himself in relation to his necessary audience. This strange dislocation haunted his strange career. Upon leaving Russia, his repertoire shrank. Disoriented, he lost touch with new music, with the very world of culture. Obsessed with what others saw, heard, and thought, he canceled concerts, took sabbaticals, spent countless months—more than anyone else would get—worrying over the editing, advertising, and promotion of his infrequent recordings. His feats, his abilities, his eagerness to please impelled a complex mating ritual—Horowitz eyeing and ignoring, stroking and rebuffing his public—bypassing music. Judging from stray comments, Horowitz himself was not unaware of the trade-offs he had settled for. "Audiences always wanted me to make a big noise," he lamented in 1965. "I could play four or five Mozart concertos and Chopin's Second, but I played the Tchaikovsky."

In America, Horowitz became known as an exemplary descendant of Anton Rubinstein, a final link in a chain of Romantic heroes also including his hero Rachmaninoff. More accurately, Horowitz was an inspired aberration, an intriguingly disfigured transplant. If he serves as a model, it is of the performer circumscribed and overshadowed by his own celebrity.

(1990)

8 · *Precision Engineering*
Glenn Gould and the Phonograph

In 1981 Glenn Gould announced that, having "pretty well exhausted" the keyboard music that interested him, he felt ready to try something besides playing the piano. Long before, he dabbled in conducting. He now hired an orchestra in Hamilton, Ontario, and rehearsed it. Then, three months before his death at age fifty in October 1982, he recorded Wagner's *Siegfried Idyll,* in the original chamber version for thirteen players, with a freelance group drawn mainly from the Toronto Symphony. Posthumously released in 1991, the recording proved a disturbing document for what it suggested both about Gould and about musical affairs in the late twentieth century.

Gould's podium debut was a private affair. He had no intention of ending his much-publicized 1964 retirement from the stage. In 1966 he had predicted that "the public concert as we know it today" would "no longer exist a century hence," that its functions would have been "entirely taken over by electronic media." In articles and interviews Gould eloquently argued that the concert format was not only anachronistic but inherently flawed. It attracted listeners who didn't want to listen. It encouraged "interpretive 'niceties' intended to woo the upper balcony." It constrained performers' repertoires and overempowered their egos.

Recordings, moreover, had in Gould's opinion engendered fresh ways of hearing. No longer was listening an exercise in communal religious devotion, complemented by the cavernous reverberation of cathedral-like spaces. The new penchant was for "analytic clarity, immediacy, and indeed almost tactile proximity." And the recording process afforded new creative possibilities. A new kind of artist, ensconced in the studio, could splice together disparate takes and reconstitute balances. A new kind of listener, ensconced in the living room, could tinker with dials, even combine excerpts from different recordings in pursuit of an "ideal performance."

Gould's McLuhanesque media prophecies—that with the demise of concerts, electronic media would convey the message—made his retirement seem timely. From another, less global perspective, the timeliness was fortuitous. Gould's aversion to public concerts was partly an aversion to the public. He was a hermit whose personal and musical eccentricities mounted as he receded from the public eye. The new kind of artist, the new kind of listener he endorsed was Gould himself—whose creations included a recording of a Bach fugue edited to alternate between two dissimilar performances.

Even Gould's verbal communications bespoke isolation. He wrote "interviews" with imaginary interlocutors. His interviews with actual others—whether in print, on radio, or on television; whether with musicians, critics, or journalists—were elaborately scripted by Gould. He read and approved Geoffrey Payzant's book *Glenn Gould: Music and Mind* before it was published, and then reviewed it. His deepening seclusion facilitated ever more profound exercises in control.

A bitter and perplexed 1989 reminiscence by the record producer Andrew Kazdin—*Glenn Gould at Work: Creative Lying*—portrays Gould as a friendless genius dominated by his mania to control, who "carefully laundered" all information about himself and stopped giving concerts partly to eliminate the risk of mishap. Though this portrait may itself be extreme—others remember Gould for his friendliness and civility—the 1982 *Siegfried Idyll* supports it. Not once do the players sound spontaneous or self-willed. No conductor on records—not Toscanini, not Karajan, not Celibidache—has so evoked an ensemble of marionette instrumentalists.

As in any Gould performance, the intentions are pellucid, and the execution is phenomenally concentrated and exact. The performance is also phenomenally slow. Throughout, the precisions of ensemble, rubato, and dynamics are superhuman. Gould weights the lines to stress and enforce Wagner's polyphony. He discourages string vibrato to impose a cooling sheen. Some may find this Wagner style hypnotic and otherworldly. I find it Martian. Even the trills are microscopically scrutinized.

The posthumous *Siegfried Idyll* release coupled Gould's podium debut with three previously issued piano performances from 1973—Gould's transcriptions of "Dawn" and "Siegfried's Rhine Journey" from *Götterdämmerung,* the *Meistersinger* Prelude, and the *Siegfried Idyll* itself. If these readings, too, are an acquired taste, acquisition is made easy: we rediscover why Gould was a tremendous pianist. All the characteristics of the orchestral *Siegfried Idyll* are present, plus others more precious. Gould's tactile engagement with the music fosters a wealth of living, breathing nuance. His trademark chiseled articulation does not preclude another, less advertised Gould trademark: all the lines, even the improbably long ones, sing.

Gould's idiosyncratic clarity of timbre here confers a sublime translucence on the *Siegfried Idyll.* His ten equalized fingers animate the contrapuntal bustle of the *Meistersinger* Prelude. These may be unconventional performances, but they capture the spirit of the text more acutely than many a more "literal" rendering. The percolating "Rhine Journey" makes us smile; it evokes Wagner's exuberantly beaming, foolishly blithe Siegfried as surely as James Levine's driven reading, at the Met, does not.

The transcriptions themselves are, needless to say, unlike anyone else's. In particular, they are unlike the Wagner transcriptions of Liszt, who knew how to make a piano sound like an orchestra. Gould makes no attempt to simulate an orchestra—as always, he rejects color washes and all other vaguenesses of articulation and sonority. Where he must sustain a violin or cello line that decays on the keyboard, he replaces the tinkling or blurry tremolos Liszt might have used in favor of internal countermelodies of his own invention.

As he once remarked in a radio interview with the CBC announcer Ken Haslam (in which Haslam's befuddled, "conversational" questions and Gould's witty answers were scripted by Gould): "I came to feel that in the Liszt transcriptions, he was too faithful to the score for his own good." To which Haslam responded: "But you don't mean to say that you played fast and loose with Wagner's textures, Glenn?" Gould: "Not 'fast and loose,' no! I simply decided that—well, for instance, that you can't hold a chord indefinitely on the piano without allowing for diminishing returns—pun intended."

Elsewhere in the interview, Gould cheerfully acknowledged overdubbing "extra hands" where the *Meistersinger* polyphony grows densest. Even if he had had audio tape to play with, Liszt, the heroic, self-sufficient virtuoso, would never have dreamed of such an expedient. But then the X-ray precision of Gould's layered renderings is not specifically "pianistic." He does not celebrate the polymorphous possibilities of the piano as a sound medium. He mainly uses the piano because it is the instrument at hand.

All of which supports the logic of Gould's becoming a conductor—albeit a hermetic one. His plans at the time of his death included recording the solo part of Beethoven's Second Piano Concerto and, on a separate occasion, its orchestral accompaniment, which he would conduct; the two performances would be combined in the studio. This, too, was a logical step for Gould. Or was it? In the privacy of his workshop, the pianist does as he pleases. But there is something grotesque about the pianist's fingers becoming human instrumentalists.

Debate over the virtues and drawbacks of "mechanical" music—a vigorous sideshow in the early days of radio and recordings—is little heard today. Gould's posthumous conducting debut powerfully reignites certain salient themes. In their different ways, Gould's overdubbing in the *Meistersinger* Prelude and his manipulation of thirteen instrumentalists in a Toronto studio demonstrate how his obsession with perfection complemented his obsession with the techniques of recorded sound. He epitomized—he espoused—the ways in which the phonograph has infiltrated how we hear and make music. In the studio, as a monitoring agent, recorded sound promotes refinements and hyper-refinements of execution. It sets standards for the concert hall. It makes a fetish of precision.

Toscanini, who set new standards of precise execution, was denounced early in his career as a human record player whose orchestras sounded like machines. The *Siegfried Idyll* recording he made with the New York Philharmonic in 1936 is surpassingly beautiful. A lyric jet stream perfectly binds its parts—and also smooths away Wagner's portraiture of the household at Tribschen: of Cosima's tender lullaby; of the six-month-old Siegfried's drowsiness and slumber. Compared with Toscanini's disembodied Wagner, Gould's performance with orchestra is actually solipsistic.

(1991)

9 · *The Worldliness of Nathan Milstein*

In 1924 Nathan Milstein and Vladimir Horowitz, then "Children of the Soviet Revolution," accepted special passports to perform abroad "for the purpose of artistic refinement and cultural propaganda." They fully expected to return to Russia—until evidence of the Stalinist nightmare reached them. And so Milstein and Horowitz eventually wound up New Yorkers.

This transplantation tellingly altered the career paths of both artists. Horowitz found himself acclaimed the world's greatest pianist—and subject to pressures that excitingly exacerbated his already high-strung artistic personality. For Milstein, whose musical temperament was as equable as Horowitz's was nervous, geographical displacement reinforced an innate and patrician detachment.

Spared the rigors of totalitarian Russia, Milstein was equally spared professional or material hardship in the West. At the same time, he was cut off from the world of culture in which he had been schooled—as a prodigy who performed the Glazunov Concerto under the composer's baton; as a pupil of the legendary violin pedagogue Leopold Auer; as the first performer in Russia of Prokofiev's D major Violin Concerto. In the United States, in England, in France, in Switzerland—all countries in which he had homes—Milstein became the complete cosmopolite, and a model of musical civility.

Milstein's violin was worldliness itself. He never forced or varnished his slender, silvery tone. He shunned the urgent vibrato of his onetime classmate Jascha Heifetz. He disdained what Virgil Thomson called the "wow effect." At top speed, his passagework was easy, clear, never out of breath. In every aspect of interpretation, he eschewed exaggeration. His very appearance, dapper and composed, was not debonair, but simply and unaffectedly aristocratic.

Two CD boxes, commemorating Milstein's death in December 1993, celebrate "The Art of Nathan Milstein" and Milstein's Bach. Assembling recordings made from 1954 to 1966, they include concertos, duo sonatas and shorter works, plus the complete Bach sonatas and partitas for unaccompanied violin. They summarize, instruct, and enthrall. They also suggest some of the limitations inherent to the most well-tempered violinist of his generation.

Of Camille Saint-Saëns it was quipped that he possessed all the attributes of a great composer save innocence; he was incurably, imperturbably urbane. Milstein's 1963 recording of Saint-Saëns's Third Concerto—a recording, that is, from his sixtieth year—is without doubt one of the most beautiful ever made by a violinist.

A performance more earnest than Milstein's would make this music sound sentimental. A more brilliant performance—from a less transcendental instrumentalist, incapable of Milstein's composure under fire—would make it sound trite. The vehemence of the concerto's opening *Allegro,* the intoxication of its luminous, swaying slow movement, the élan and manqué religiosity of its tarantella-and-chorale finale—all, in Milstein's hands, are poised, but perfectly, between passion and refinement. The result is transformative: an exercise in elegance and craftsmanship become sublime.

In his 1990 autobiography, *From Russia to the West* (written with Solomon Volkov), Milstein loftily dismissed conductors as an irrelevance—an opinion comprehensible from a musician whose musicality meshed so completely, and necessarily, with instrumental finesse. Paradoxically, Milstein's own concerto recordings suffer from the absence of more collaborative partnership. (I once had occasion to observe Milstein rehearse the Bruch G minor Concerto; he dictated countless details of tempo, rubato, and phrasing directly to the concertmaster.)

In Saint-Saëns, this hardly matters: nothing more is asked for than Anatole Fistoulari's finely attuned accompaniment. In the Brahms Concerto, however, Fistoulari's deference is problematic. And yet, violinistically, Milstein's Brahms is a wonderful refreshment; he levitates the ponderous finale. In the rondos of the Beethoven and Dvořák Concertos, Milstein again dances his way through music others make more strenuous or brilliant. And no other violinist sings the *Canzonetta* of the Tchaikovsky Concerto as intimately—or takes such pleasure, generally, in playing quietly, and with so delicately nuanced a vibrato.

Of the recorded duo sonatas and miniatures, it is the miniatures that take stock of the player. In Sarasate's *Introduction and Tarantella,* where a demonic virtuosity is relevant, Milstein can sound bland. In Kreisler's *Praeludium and Allegro,* he is supreme. This piece, as he purveys it, is about the violin, which he loves simply and sincerely. His identification with his instrument—he is said to have rarely put it down; it was an appendage of his conversation—forges an invigorating unity. Listening to such playing is as tireless an activity as the playing itself.

If Milstein's capacity to reveal his art through the cameos of a Tchaikovsky, Wieniawski, or Kreisler suggests an old-fashioned practitioner of the Russian school, in other respects he is hard to place. His early recordings reveal a strikingly "modern" approach for the 1930s. Unlike such Auer students as Mischa Elman, he never teases the line and only infrequently slides from note to note. And he was decades ahead of his time for championing the solo violin works of Bach, which he began acquiring and performing at a tender age.

The affinity is understandable. Milstein adopted no special Baroque style. He did not strive to make Bach sound meaningful. His feeling for the dance, his purity of timbre, his abhorrence of artifice all contributed to an enduring vision of the solo sonatas and partitas. He recorded all of them twice; the 1954–56 cycle, on EMI, is brisker, more robust, and more extroverted than the 1973 set, on Deutsche Grammophon.

Different listeners will bring much different expectations to these performances; personally, I look for more interiority in Bach, conducive to more explicit peaks and valleys. Perhaps it would be accurate to suggest that Milstein used Bach to celebrate the violin (in contrast to his Central European antipode Joseph Szigeti, who used his violin to probe Bach and Beethoven).

In fact, a 1993 videocassette, "Nathan Milstein: Master of Invention," records Milstein's touching confession that he loves the violin "more than music." Directed by Christopher Nupen, the tape also documents Milstein's final recital, at age eighty-two. (He continued to appear with orchestra until a fluke hand injury ended his career two years later.) No previous violinist commanded anything like Milstein's prowess at so advanced an age—corroboration of the complete and natural fluency of his technical gift.

Unfortunately, Nupen's documentary includes no footage from Milstein's prime, which lasted well into the 1970s. And the interviews postdate his retirement. Milstein without his fiddle seems an uncomfortably naked presence. His exchanges with Nupen, and with Pinchas Zukerman, are strained and superficial. His ideal interlocutor would have been his friend of fifty years, Gregor Piatigorsky, who died in 1976 and who was a world-class raconteur.

Piatigorsky's autobiography, *Cellist,* is the kind that even musicians used to write before television and video, a memento of less hurried times when books weren't dictated into tape recorders and when a well-told tale, or a phrase well turned, was more savored than a talk show date. Of "Nathanchik," Piatigorsky wrote:

His quick movements, lively eyes and shiny black hair, and his strong, medium-sized frame suggested youth that would stay with him forever.... So spontaneous and harmless was he that one hated to be critical of anything he said.... Nathan had no trace of restlessness. He was self-sufficient, unperturbed and always neat; his friends, his surroundings, his violin, his exquisite cashmere sweaters, all existed to augment his pleasure.

The "self-sufficiency" of Milstein's art, its civilizing poise and affirmative wholeness, its immunity to fanfare were timeless qualities evocative of older times. "Composers and performers remind me more and more of bazaar hawkers or clowns," he wrote in *From Russia to the West.* "They try to lure the public and sell off their wares.... I rarely despair, but sometimes in the middle of this vanity fair I just feel like giving up: Have all standards been changed irrevocably?"

Milstein remembered the excitement of Monte Carlo in the late 1920s, where he came upon Diaghilev, Stravinsky, and Lifar and, with Horowitz, enjoyed the cuisine of the Palace Hotel—which decades later he discovered emptied and boarded up. He recalled his many late nights with Balanchine at the Russian Tea Room in New York, before it turned into "a catastrophe . . . like eating at Howard Johnson's." And he savored his early memories of Odessa and St. Petersburg, of the ferment and refinements of pre-revolutionary Russia. Among Russian writers, he preferred Chekhov, of whom he said: "Reading him is like being in a hospitable Russian house, where you are given soothing, fragrant tea and the conversation is gentle and wise."

From another artist, such retrospection might sound smug. But Milstein's detachment, reinforced by the circumstances of a benign exile, was uplifting. Only at the end of his life did his worldliness prove out of date.

(1993)

10 · *The Teachings of Leonard Bernstein*

Virgil Thomson once called Leonard Bernstein "the ideal explainer of music, both classical and modern." Bernstein explained more than that. The dozens of programs he wrote and hosted for television—including the twenty-five Young People's Concerts now available on video cassette—range effortlessly from Bach to jazz, rock, and Broadway. As TV time capsules, they also explore an incidental topic scarcely apparent when these shows were new: Bernstein himself as the embodiment of America's musical aspirations and disappointments over a period of two decades.

Before World War I American musical pedagogy routinely stressed the ability to read music, to play an instrument, and to perceive sonata form and other elements of musical structure. In *How to Listen to Music,* reprinted thirty times between 1896 and 1924, Henry Krehbiel began by chastising the reader's ignorance; he bluntly conceded his willingness "to seem unamiable to the amateur while arguing the need of even so mild a stimulant" as the book in hand. The "music appreciators" who followed between the wars, by comparison, came swathed in smiles. They tutored a broader, more passive audience than Krehbiel's amateurs: an enlarged middle-class constituency for high culture attuned to such 1920s popularizers as Will Durant and Hendrik van Loon.

George Marek, in *How to Listen to Music over the Radio,* reassured in 1937: "You can enjoy a Beethoven symphony without being able to read notes, without knowing who Beethoven was, when he lived, or what he tried to express." Olin Downes, the chief music critic of the *New York Times,* echoed: "The listener does not have to be a tutored man or a person technically versed in the intricacies of the art of composition to understand perfectly well what the orchestra [is] saying to him." In 1949 Marek wrote a *Good Housekeeping Guide to Musical Enjoyment*—a volume incidentally reflecting the homemaker's migration from the parlor spinet to the family phonograph—which prescribed no composer later than Wagner or Verdi.

Krehbiel, the lordly dean of New York's turn-of-the-century music critics, pondered how to create a distinctively American musical high culture. He urged contemporary American composers to study the music of African Americans and American Indians. He advocated opera in English as a catalyst toward an American operatic tradition. The music appreciators had no such concerns; attracted to foreign accents, they appointed, and sanctified, a pantheon of European masters. Paralleling Marek's advice to adults, a textbook for children preached: "It is difficult to study Beethoven, for his genius is colossal, his sublimity so overwhelming that it compels one's awe and reverence as well as one's admiration." Paradoxically, the popularizers fostered a new elitism: to participate in the exclusive aura of Great Music became a democratic privilege.

America's own music was ignored. One purpose of music education was to inoculate against jazz and other popular forms. Antipathy to modernism, and to contemporary culture generally, deprived the popularizers of living hero composers. Instead, they deified performers, beginning with Arturo Toscanini, whose repertoire fortuitously replicated the music appreciation canon.

Whatever the pedagogic deficiencies of music appreciation, it succeeded admirably, and not so incidentally, as a marketing strategy. Concentrating on reputation and personality—the Great

Composers, the Great Performers—it broadened the grounds for popular appeal and amassed a permanent catalog of durable merchandise. Its commercial strategies were nakedest at David Sarnoff's National Broadcasting Corporation, whose Radio Corporation of America commanded both the nation's largest radio network and the leading record label for classical music. NBC/RCA, whose employees eventually included Marek and Toscanini, was an eager purveyor of educational materials keyed to Victor artists and recordings. The popular *Victor Book of the Symphony* (1934) included "A List of Modern Victor Recordings of Symphonic Music"; Victor's *Form in Music* (1945) incorporated a "Minimum List of RCA Victor Records." But Sarnoff's most prestigious, most influential music-educational undertaking was NBC's *Music Appreciation Hour,* a weekly daytime radio series begun in 1928 and said to reach seven million students in seventy thousand schools by 1937. Its host, Walter Damrosch, was the quintessential music appreciation broadcaster.

Damrosch came to the United States from Breslau with his father, Leopold, a gifted conductor who helped to introduce Wagner at the Metropolitan Opera. When Leopold died in 1885, Walter, aged twenty-three, vied to take his place. Though at best a pedestrian musician—it is unlikely that he could have sustained a major career in Europe—he capitalized on his entrepreneurial vigor, German origin, and good looks. An advantageous marriage allied him with the socially powerful and well-to-do. When the Met lost interest in him, he was able to form his own Damrosch Opera Company. When the New York Philharmonic passed him by, he reorganized his own New York Symphony. When in 1928 the New York Symphony was absorbed by the Philharmonic, he was hired by Sarnoff, who called him "America's leading ambassador of music understanding and music appreciation."

Damrosch's grandfatherly persona—he was eighty when the *Music Appreciation Hour* ended in 1942—made him the perfect embodiment of "serious music." He began his lessons by intoning "Good morning, my dear children!" His repertoire was more varied than Toscanini's—but only up to a point. Leopold Stokowski, who knew how to excite children, proposed broadcasting "modernistic" music so they could "develop a liking for it." Damrosch issued a press release "deeply deploring" the plan. "Children should not be confused by experiments," he wrote.

Leonard Bernstein, at twenty-three, was already Serge Koussevitzky's assistant at Tanglewood the year Damrosch's lessons went off the air. A year later, in 1943, he replaced Bruno Walter on short notice with the New York Philharmonic, and his conducting career was launched. Between 1944 and 1953 he also composed *Fancy Free, On the Town, The Age of Anxiety, Trouble in Tahiti,* and *Wonderful Town.* The Serenade for Violin, Strings, Harp, and Percussion was finished in 1954—the year of his first telecast for *Omnibus* (then television's most important cultural showcase, hosted by Alistair Cooke). He was young, irreverent, eclectic—as "American" as Damrosch was "European." He swiftly established a pedagogical agenda that swept aside what Virgil Thomson called "the music appreciation racket." Far from sanctifying famous music, he dismantled it to see how it worked, or juxtaposed it with popular music, which he adored. He campaigned for modern music and American music.

The diversity of Bernstein's curriculum, pursued through fifty-three televised Young People's Concerts, twenty-one programs for *Omnibus, Ford Presents,* and *Lincoln Presents,* and six televised Norton lectures given at Harvard, was not wholly unprecedented. Olga Samaroff, once Stokowski's wife, had endorsed "modern creative music" in her 1935 *Layman's Book of Music.* In 1939 Aaron Copland, in *What to Listen for in Music,* had taught that "real lovers of music are unwilling to have their musical enjoyment confined to the overworked period of the three B's." But Bernstein, who first heard an orchestral concert only at the age of fourteen, and who once, as Lenny Amber, had supported himself arranging pop songs and transcribing jazz improvisations, was far fresher, more varied in scope and resource.

And yet Bernstein's achievement as an explainer of music was short-lived. No master educator has taken his place. His "young people" have not musically inculcated their young. Nor has any American public or cable television network agreed to rebroadcast Bernstein's Young People's Concerts, as they are today rebroadcast in Europe and Japan. Bernstein the teacher already seems an anachronism. His video lessons help to explain what happened.

Bernstein's second Young People's Concert, "What Is American Music?" broadcast February 1, 1958, is a natural starting point. It poses a problem: compared to Poland, Italy, Ireland, Spain, Hungary, or Russia, countries whose music Bernstein briefly samples, the United States lacks a common folk music. "Don't forget, America is a very new country, compared to all those European ones. We're not even two hundred years old yet! . . . We're still a baby." Bernstein answers the problem with a spunky polemic, a schematized history based on his Harvard bachelor's thesis of nineteen years before.

The first "really serious" American music, he explains, began about seventy-five years ago. "At that time the few American composers we did have were imitating European composers, like Brahms and Liszt and Wagner. . . . We might call that the kindergarten period of American music." Bernstein here conducts a snatch of George Chadwick's *Melpomene* Overture—"straight European stuff." Next, around the turn of the century, "American composers were beginning to feel funny about not writing American-*sounding* music." Dvořák's *New World* Symphony (1893) proposed seeking African-American and American Indian source materials. But the result sounded Czech, not American. "In spite of this Dvořák made a big impression on the American composers of his time, and they all got excited, too, and began to write hundreds of so-called American pieces with Indian and Negro melodies in them. It became a disease, almost an epidemic." This "grade school" period is exemplified by Edward MacDowell's *Indian* Suite—"I still can't say that it sounds very American to me!"—and Henry Gilbert's New Orleans vignette, *Dance in Place Congo.*

After World War I came "high school." By this time, "something new and very special had come into American music. . . . Jazz had been born and that changed everything. Because at last there was something like an American folk music that belonged to *all* Americans." Even serious composers couldn't keep jazz out of their ears. Bernstein illustrates with bits of Copland's *Music for the Theater* and Gershwin's *Rhapsody in Blue*—and also, by way of demonstrating jazz's transatlantic reach, of Stravinsky's *Ragtime.* But Copland and Gershwin remained in high school: they "were still being American *on purpose.*" Only in the 1930s was the jazz influence integrated, so that Americans "just wrote music, and it came out American all by itself." This was "college," and its students included Roger Sessions, whose Chorale Prelude for organ incorporates syncopated accents no European could have written.

"Mature" American contemporary concert music, Bernstein continues, embraces certain personality traits. One is youth: "loud, strong, wildly optimistic"—as in William Schuman's *American Festival* Overture. Another is rugged "pioneer energy"— as in Roy Harris's Third Symphony. A third is a kind of loneliness, evoking "the great wide open spaces that our big country is full of"—as in Copland's *Billy the Kid.* "Then there's a kind of sweet, simple, sentimental quality that gets into our music" from hymn singing—as in Virgil Thomson's *The Mother of Us All.*

Finally, "we have another kind of sentimentality . . . that comes out of our popular songs, a sort of crooning pleasure, like taking a long, delicious, warm bath"—as in a tune from Randall Thompson's Second Symphony, "almost like a song Perry Como sings." In fact, America's strength is its "many-sidedness." "We've taken it all in: French, Dutch, German, Scotch, Scandinavian, Italian, and all the rest, and learned it from one another, borrowed it, stolen it, cooked it all up in a melting pot. So what our composers are finally nourished on is a folk music that is probably the richest in the world, and all of it is American." The hour ends with the final pages of Copland's Third Symphony, conducted by the composer himself.

While not every Young People's Concert considers American music, Bernstein typically draws on contemporary culture, high and low. Dealing with Beethoven or Gershwin, Stravinsky or Simon and Garfunkel, he is of his own time and place: the America of the 1960s. Partly because he came relatively late to classical music, he feels challenged to mediate between Old World and New. The urgency of his need to place himself as an American classical musician reinforces the energy of his delivery. One can disagree with how he answers this need—to my mind, he underrates Chadwick and other kindergarten composers, and overpraises such college graduates as Schuman and Harris. He fails to account for the "pre-college" achievement of Charles Ives. He succumbs to a naive enthusiasm for his own enthusiasm. But his communicative passion is irresistible; in the heat of engagement, what he says matters—and mattered to his young people, even when his ideas sailed over their heads—because we feel sure it matters to him.

This is one way of suggesting that Bernstein is never a patronizing or sanctimonious teacher. It also suggests the degree to which his style is self-referential—and that this is a strength. The music appreciators were sensitive to how America looked to European eyes. Bernstein, who cannot be embarrassed, directly and familiarly engages composers from other countries. For him, the United States is the place to be: young, versatile, breathless with possibility.

Music appreciation ranked the masterpieces of Mozart and Beethoven in order of holiness. Bernstein's canons, by comparison, are purposely unholy. Investigating "What Makes Music Symphonic?" (December 13, 1958), he illustrates sequential progression with Tchaikovsky, Mozart, Gershwin, and Elvis Presley. In "What Is a Mode?" (November 23, 1966), his examples include plainsong (as sung by the New York Philharmonic), Sibelius's Sixth, "Along Comes Mary," and "Secret Agent Man." Exploring

"Folk Music in the Concert Hall" (April 9, 1961), he offers the finale of Ives's Second Symphony. Examining "What Is Orchestration?" (March 8, 1958), he tests the sound of a trumpet in a flute solo by Debussy and has a viola play a Gershwin clarinet riff; he illustrates the woodwinds in the "wonderful cool colors" of Stravinsky's *Symphonies of Wind Instruments*; he contrasts "America the Beautiful" on the violin's D string versus the G string ("richer and fatter"); and he tops off the hour with *Bolero,* whose tune he likens to "high-class hootchy-kootchy music." In "The Sound of an Orchestra" (December 14, 1965), he juxtaposes the "absolute clarity, like a perfect photograph," of the "Royal March" from Stravinsky's *Soldier's Tale*—a "sort of pop art," "like a comic strip"—with the "direct, strong, and yet casual" trumpet solos of *An American in Paris,* and the "freewheeling, easy" fiddling of the "Hoedown" from Copland's *Rodeo.* He devotes a program to "Jazz in the Concert Hall" (March 11, 1964), and another to "The Latin-American Spirit" (March 8, 1963), in which he broadens his embrace of American diversity.

Part of Bernstein's identification with America, his insistence on juxtaposing an American presence beside Old World art, is his identification with American youth. His admiration for pop and rock—from "All Shook Up," which he bellows, to "Eleanor Rigby," which he croons—is not even ironic. In "Bach Transmogrified" (April 27, 1969), he sympathetically considers the "new Bach rage": a "switched-on" synthesizer performance framed by the New York Rock 'n' Roll Ensemble's sung adaptation of the Fifth Brandenburg, Lukas Foss's nightmare vision of the E major Violin Partita in *Baroque* Variations, and Leopold Stokowski's technicolored orchestration of the "Little" G minor Fugue, conducted by Stokowski himself.

"Berlioz Takes a Trip" (May 25, 1969) presents the *Symphonie fantastique* as "the first psychedelic symphony in history," an opium dream not "very different from modern days." Movement one, "Visions and Passions," is "the portrait of a nervous wreck." Where the *idée fixe,* the theme of the beloved, growls in the low strings while woodwinds and horns "are heaving a series of heart-breaking sighs," the result is "a perfect picture of the agony of jealous rage." Where, in movement three, following a nightmare of panic and terror, a piping shepherd is answered by hollow distant thunder, the result is "a dramatic picture of the pain of loneliness that has probably never been equaled, not even by the most neurotic composers of our century." Trip's end, "Witches' Sabbath," is not melodramatic but documentary: "Berlioz tells it like it is. . . . You take a trip, you wind up screaming at your own funeral."*

This teaching style—Bernstein as the mirror of Berlioz, the 1960s as the measure of all things—is not an irritant because Bernstein's excess seems unfeigned; we do not feel hectored. Another, more enduring, more self-revealing portrait is "Who is Gustav Mahler?" (February 7, 1960). Mahler's uniqueness, Bernstein argues, is his ability to "recapture the pure emotions of childhood," oscillating between extremes of happiness and gloom. Mahler is at the same time Romantic and modern. He is both conductor and composer. He is rooted yet marginal. Torn between East and West, he is Jewish, he is Austrian, he absorbs Slavic and Chinese influences. Mahler is an exuberant and depressive man-child, a twentieth-century American eclectic.

Generally, Bernstein's earlier shows are pedagogically the most ambitious, and the most concerned with issues of American identity. They are likely to consider such general subjects as "What Does Music Mean?" "What Is Classical Music?" and "Humor in Music." The later shows incorporate fewer contemporary or American works. Bernstein is more likely to play and discuss a single

---

*Here, and elsewhere, I transcribe the actual scripts, not the edited versions in *Leonard Bernstein's Young People's Concerts* (New York: Anchor Books, 1993), which has Bernstein preach: "Take a tip from Berlioz: that music is all you need for the wildest trip you can take, to hell and back. With drugs you might make it, but you might not make it back."

big piece from the week's subscription concerts. "Berlioz Takes a Trip" is one example; others examine Strauss's *Also sprach Zarathustra,* Liszt's *Faust* Symphony, and—Bernstein's final Young People's Concert, telecast March 26, 1972—Holst's *The Planets.*

By this time, Bernstein's best television work was behind him. I refer not only to the early Young People's Concerts but to the programs he wrote and hosted for *Omnibus, Ford Presents,* and *Lincoln Presents* between 1954 and 1962 (and which are not at this writing destined for the home video market). Bernstein's debut studio telecast, "Beethoven's Fifth Symphony" (November 14, 1954), demonstrates a more elaborate, more creative use of the medium than the Young People's Concerts (all of which were concert hall presentations for a live audience). Bernstein stands on a huge reproduction of page one of Beethoven's score and admires its famous four-note motto underfoot. To illustrate the twelve different instruments Beethoven employs, Bernstein has a dozen musicians stand on the appropriate staves; to illustrate how the conductor's eye must "follow all the instruments simultaneously," he has the musicians walk slowly across the page.

Partly because he need not present himself as an orchestral conductor, Bernstein in the studio explores an even more catholic range of subjects than he does for young people. His most personal investigations are of musical theater: the linked worlds of Broadway, operetta, and opera. An ingenious example is "The American Musical Comedy" (October 7, 1956). At the age of thirty-eight, Bernstein on television is suave and yet a neophyte; his slightly fidgety excitement—a restless cigarette dangles from his mouth—complements a touching innocence. "The glittering world of musical theater is an enormous field that includes everything from your nephew's high school pageant to *Götterdämmerung,*" he begins.

And somehow in that great mass of song and dance and drama lies something called the American musical comedy—a magic phrase. We seem to be addicted to it; we

pay enormous sums to attend it; we discuss it at breakfast
and at cocktail parties with a passion otherwise reserved
for elections and the Dodgers. We anticipate a new musical comedy of Rodgers and Hammerstein or of Frank Loes-
ser with the same excitement and partisan feeling as Milan
used to await a new Puccini opera, or Vienna the latest
Brahms symphony. We hear on all sides that America has
given the world a new form—unique, vital, inimitable.
Yet no one seems to be able to tell us what this phenomenon is. Why is *Guys and Dolls* unique? What makes *South
Pacific* different? Why can't Europe imitate *Pajama Game*?
Is *My Fair Lady* a milestone along the road to a new form
of art?

Carried away by the audacity of such sincere hyperbole, Bernstein pokes fun at Europe. In a musical show, he explains, dialogue
would impart that "chicken is up three cents a pound." In opera,
where everything is sung, this becomes the business of recitative—and Bernstein sings, à la Mozart, "Susanna, I have something terrible to tell you. I've just been talking to the butcher,
and he tells me that the price of chicken has gone up three cents a
pound! Please don't be too depressed, dear." There follows a pocket
history of American musical theater, a polemic of New World
promise and achievement anticipating "What Is American Music?" some sixteen months later. Bernstein starts by sampling
"You Naughty, Naughty Men" and other primitive ditties from
the first American hit musical, *The Black Crook* of 1866. Offenbach, Johann Strauss, and Gilbert and Sullivan led Americans toward operetta; one result was Victor Herbert's *Naughty Marietta,
Eileen,* and *The Red Mill*—in Bernstein's opinion, shows achieving
"a new level of musical accomplishment," and yet "fancy and
somewhat remote from the audience's experience."

Meanwhile, "just across the street," the revue was a more vernacular entertainment infused with jazz. This "childhood" stage
of American musical theater ripened to adolescence in the 1920s,

whose composers, a "sensational array," included Irving Berlin, Jerome Kern, Vincent Youmans, Cole Porter, Richard Rodgers, and Gershwin. A decade later—"young manhood"—Broadway began to fuse operetta and popular song. Here Bernstein and his singers contrast the similarly plotted first act finales of *The Mikado* and Gershwin's *Of Thee I Sing,* switching back and forth, episode by episode, to argue an equivalent technical mastery. Finally, the high/low synthesis, an American specialty, is consummated by Gershwin, Marc Blitzstein, and Kurt Weill—as well as by Rodgers and Hammerstein, whose *South Pacific* attains a "new sophistication" in the sung introduction—a sort of double soliloquy, neither song nor recitative—to "Some Enchanted Evening." All this conditions Bernstein's culminating hyper-claims—that "for the last fifteen years we have been enjoying the greatest period our musical theater has ever known," that "a new form has been born," that

> We are in a historical position now similar to that of the popular musical theater in Germany just before Mozart came along. In 1750, the big attraction was what they called the *Singspiel,* which was the *Annie Get Your Gun* of its day, star comic and all. This popular form took the leap to a work of art through the genius of Mozart. After all, the *Magic Flute* is a *Singspiel*; only it's by Mozart. We are in the same position; all we need is for our Mozart to come along. . . . And this event can happen any second. It's almost as though it is our moment in history, as if there is a historical necessity that gives us such a wealth of creative talent at this precise time.

(A mere second later, the following August, *West Side Story*—another Bernstein version of the American melting pot—opened on Broadway.)

An inspired sequel to "American Musical Comedy" is "The Drama of *Carmen,*" for *Ford Presents* (March 11, 1962). Bernstein juxtaposes the interpolated dialogue of the original score with the recitatives composed by Ernest Guiraud after Bizet's death, and universally adopted by opera houses in Europe and the United States. Guiraud, as Bernstein demonstrates, simplified details of plot and characterization. Unlike Guiraud's prissy Don José, Bizet's José has murdered a man. And Bizet's Carmen, more complex than Guiraud's, is a "true beatnik" who "sees life as a drama." What is more, Bizet's way of moving from speech to song—"I won't say a word," Carmen tells Zuniga by way of launching a wordless *chanson*—opens a creative synapse. The subtext of Bernstein's exercise, of course, is that the real *Carmen* is not grand opera, but a near cousin to American musical comedy. Its use of dialogue furnishes expressive possibilities foreclosed once the alternation of speech and song is abandoned. By way of appreciating French *opéra comique,* Bernstein celebrates Broadway.

And yet his final television classroom, eleven years later, reveals a different Bernstein: embattled, self-conscious, ambivalent. Enchanted evenings of Rodgers and Hammerstein seem long forgotten. Mahler, once a symbol of "pure emotions," now symbolizes death. In the intervening decade, Bernstein had changed; and so had his America.

Bernstein's six Norton lectures, delivered at Harvard University in 1973, were televised three years later and are now available on video cassette. The collective title, borrowed from Charles Ives, is "The Unanswered Question"—which to Bernstein means: "Whither music in our time?" His answer incorporates an overview of music history from Mozart to Schoenberg and Stravinsky. A second component of the lectures is an exercise in "musico-linguistics," applying Chomskyan language theory to the phonology, syntax, and semantics of symphonies and tone poems. And, thirdly, there are big chunks of music in performance, with Bernstein conducting the Boston Symphony and (in one instance) the Berlin Philharmonic. Otherwise, the setting is intimate: a piano, a desk, a roomful of Harvard students and faculty types.

Never before or after did Bernstein appear so uncomfortable on screen. It is only partly because the lectures were prepared helter-skelter, from one meeting to the next. Bernstein struggles visibly toward his accustomed aplomb: repeatedly, he scratches his ear, musses his hair, pinches his nose. A new style of address, laced with fancy phrases ("the diatonic containment of chromaticism"), sits awkwardly beside a more colloquial, more "American" mode. Affirming belief in "mind, heart, and spirit," Bernstein feels the need to apologize for such "old-fashioned words." "Why am I doing this?" becomes a recurrent refrain—another unanswered question. "What's the relevance of all this musico-linguistics?" begins lecture two. "Isn't it a flagrant case of [intellectual] elitism?" Bernstein here argues that the analogy to language potentially furnishes "a way of speaking about music with intelligent but nonprofessional music lovers who don't know a stretto from a diminished fifth." On other occasions, he contends that structural linguistics illuminates music in new ways for professional and nonprofessional alike.

In previous public incarnations, Bernstein seemed fortified by his versatility and eclecticism, secure in his identity as an American classical musician-cum-Broadway composer. His new uncertainty is a distraction, not a charming self-effacement: he strains for intellectual credibility as an original thinker. Chomsky is his Harvard calling card. The terminology of structural linguistics spreads a scholarly patina. And Chomsky's belief in a universal and innate linguistic grammar leads in a direction Bernstein wants to go—toward a universal and innate musical grammar grounded in tonality, whose gravitational pull he considers irreplaceable.

Bernstein plunges in courageously. A note, he suggests, can be equated with a phoneme, a motive with a morpheme, a musical phrase with a word, a musical section with a clause, a musical movement with a sentence. But he stumbles when, in music, "words" overlap as they cannot in speech. Another attempt: a musical motive (Bernstein uses "Fate" from Wagner's *Ring*) is a noun phrase whose notes are like letters, and whose chordal and rhythmic modifiers resemble adjectives and verbs. On further consideration, however, language possesses both communicative and aesthetic functions, whereas music is only aesthetic. Ordinary sentences, therefore, lack musical equivalents, the linguistic parallel to music being poetry. This inference, patiently pursued, yields results so complicated they parody Bernstein's intention to explain music to nonprofessionals. That the first melodic downbeat of Mozart's Fortieth Symphony falls on a "weak" bar, a professional insight the Bernstein of *Omnibus* might have imparted with sleight of hand, in the heavy hands of Professor Bernstein becomes an observation of numbing complexity, requiring charts with pyramids and terms like "deep structure" and "syntactic truth."

As the lectures progress, Bernstein in fact jettisons Chomsky. The less he strives for originality, the more authentic he becomes. He observes that, after Mozart, the increasingly chromatic language of Beethoven, Berlioz, Wagner, and Debussy creates heightened possibilities for a delightful or menacing ambiguity. The Prelude to *Tristan und Isolde* keeps the listener guessing—is it tonal or atonal, anchored or unmoored? The *Prelude to the Afternoon of a Faun* is—like the Mallarmé poem that inspired it—a "last ditch stand" of tonal and syntactic containment. Bernstein's instructive analyses of these pieces, of the controlled ambiguities arising from a dialectic of chromatic deviation and diatonic repose, are purely musical, with Chomsky laid on afterward as intellectual icing.

The strongest of the six Norton lectures is the fifth, "The Twentieth Century Crisis." Here Bernstein is most in his element and furthest from Harvard. To solve the crisis of fading tonality, Schoenberg logically proceeded to atonality, which he systematized by employing twelve-tone rows. But this was an "artificial language." In fact, Schoenberg constantly reverted to an explicit or implied tonality; he "loved music with such passion" he could not overthrow its necessary foundation. A "nostalgic yearning for the deep structures" of diatonic music, Bernstein claims, haunts such works as the Opus 23 Piano Pieces and Third String Quartet, with their melodic fourths and fifths and covert tonic-dominant harmonic gestures—qualities that crucially contribute to making this music "beautiful and moving." It could actually be said that *all* music "is ultimately and basically tonal, even when it's nontonal."

Even so, Schoenberg's implicit "tonal" practice embodies ambiguities that exceed our intuitive grasp. The truly emblematic twentieth-century composer is Mahler, whose attempts to relinquish tonality are reluctant and incomplete, and whose nostalgia for past practice is overt and tragic. Mahler's Ninth Symphony, his "last will and testament," shows "that ours is the century of death, and Mahler is its musical prophet." That is the "real reason" Mahler's music suffered posthumous neglect—it was, Bernstein says, "telling something too dreadful to hear." The Ninth Symphony embodies three kinds of death—Mahler's own, which he knew was imminent; the death of tonality, "which for him meant the death of music itself"; and "the death of society, of our Faustian culture." And yet this music, like all great art, paradoxically reanimates us.

Bernstein's final Norton lecture considers Stravinsky, whom he admires for his sustained (if ultimately abrogated) allegiance to tonality, for his eclecticism, and for the nourishment he drew from vernacular sources, including jazz. For Bernstein, Stravinsky's embarrassed response to direct emotional expression achieves a paradoxical Romantic poignance, "speaking for all us frightened children."

While Bernstein concludes by prophesying a more wholesome musical future, a "new eclecticism" grounded in tonality, his once boyish optimism seems freighted with Old World gravitas and gloom. Even without the strained appeal to Chomsky, his sanguine rhetoric is strained, and so are its interpretive props. His readings of Schoenberg and Stravinsky, both of whom are shown to gain power from an inadvertent Romanticism, are impossibly tendentious; he exaggerates the place of poignance—of poignant tonal yearnings, of poignant reticence—in their emotional worlds. And the Mahler-equals-Bernstein equation this time fails to convince: we know at a glance that the Twentieth-Century Crisis of the fifth lecture is also Bernstein's crisis, with an offstage American history of its own.

In 1964–65, on sabbatical from the New York Philharmonic, Bernstein had experimented with serialism, and, by his own account, wrote "a lot of music, twelve-tone music and avant-garde music of various kinds," only to discard it. As a theater composer, he never repeated the success of *West Side Story.* The early Serenade for Violin, Strings, Harp, and Percussion remained his most successful concert work. Writing in *The New York Times* in 1965, he mulled "the ancient cliché that the certainty of one's knowledge decreases in proportion to thought and experience," pondered "the present crisis in composition," asked if tonality were forever dead, and worried that orchestras would "become museums of the past." A 1967 television interview in conjunction with the Philharmonic's 125th birthday revealed a spent and disillusioned Bernstein; he had recently announced that he would relinquish his music directorship as of 1969. Thirteen years later, addressing the American Symphony Orchestra League, Bernstein complained of the "apathy and joylessness" of orchestral musicians.

Bernstein's mentor Koussevitzky had forecast: "The next Beethoven vill from Colorado come." But neither Bernstein nor anyone else wrote the Great American Symphony. Meanwhile, the Broadway that Bernstein had exuberantly praised, whose stellar practitioners he had compared to Puccini in Milan and Brahms in Vienna, had not proved the boulevard to greatness he had predicted. American popular music—not only jazz, but 1960s and 1970s rock, which he loved for its vitality and inventiveness— had in his opinion also lost its way. A new popular culture, with which he could not identify, erased the high-culture berths once reserved for classical music on commercial television. "Mediocrity and art-mongering increasingly uglify our lives," he complained in the Norton lectures. Outside music, the demise of the Kennedy White House, in which he had been a frequent guest, tarnished his dreams for America. His famous 1970 fundraising party for the Black Panther defense fund, savagely ridiculed by Tom Wolfe as "radical chic," again caught him out of step.

On *Omnibus,* in his Young People's Concerts, Bernstein had excitedly chronicled the growing up of American classical music and musical theater. "All we need is our Mozart to come along." It could "happen any second." It never did.

Bernstein's relative disillusionment might have signaled the relative derailment of his career. Nothing of the kind occurred. Rather, his career was rerouted in the only possible direction: Europe. In particular, Vienna—the city of Beethoven and Mahler—exerted an ineluctable pull. In Vienna he led *Falstaff, Der Rosenkavalier, Fidelio,* and his own *A Quiet Place.* The Vienna Philharmonic supplanted the New York Philharmonic as the orchestra with which he most often toured and recorded. And he was lionized in Vienna as Americans—or Viennese—would never have revered one of their own.

Visiting the Soviet Union in 1959 with the New York Philharmonic, Bernstein had discovered America in Russia and Russia in America. At a Moscow concert beamed to the United States, he juxtaposed Copland and Shostakovich and discovered a common heroism, humor, and candor. A decade later, in Vienna, Bernstein no longer championed America. Bernstein the composer and public educator dropped from view. On television, he turned up on a different kind of program: not sui generis *Omnibus* specials, Young People's Concerts, or Norton lectures, but symphonies by Mozart, Beethoven, Brahms, and Mahler—the same Great Performances routine associated with Karajan.

Bernstein's new identity was international. All his major concerts were videotaped or filmed. Jetting between Vienna, London, Tel Aviv, Rome, New York, he trailed a cornucopia of CDs, cassettes, souvenir books, and coffee mugs. The more ubiquitous he became, the more elusive became the American Lenny of yesteryear. He increasingly acquired a reputation for eccentricity.

The retrenchment to Great Performer worked for Bernstein because he happened to retrench into a great conductor. Perhaps the cradling traditions of the Vienna Philharmonic and its Musikverein taught and inspired him as the New York Philharmonic and Lincoln Center had not. Perhaps he had merely needed to grow older, or to concentrate his talents more narrowly. In any event, his later recordings thrive on a Furtwänglerian mastery of long-range harmonic tension and release—an interpretive largesse not apparent in the Young People's Concerts of the 1960s.

Bernstein never abandoned his pedagogic gift. He continued to teach young musicians in Fontainebleau, Sapporo, Schleswig-Holstein, and Tanglewood. But, aside from sometimes introducing his own television performances, he stopped teaching laymen and their offspring. He last appeared at a Lincoln Center children's event on March 14, 1984—the sixtieth anniversary celebration of the New York Philharmonic Young People's Concerts. He conducted but, incongruously, did not speak. A member of the Philharmonic's staff confided afterward that, since Bernstein was "crazy," he could not be trusted to address an audience of children. "We would have no control over what he might say."

Another bizarre Bernstein event was a performance of Mahler's *Resurrection* Symphony at Avery Fisher Hall in April 1987—a sublime concert confused by its denouement. Lauren Bacall stepped to a microphone to present Bernstein with the "Albert Schweitzer Music Award." The popping flashbulbs of this rude ceremony epitomized the artist upstaged by his own celebrity.

The teachings of Leonard Bernstein chart a process of disengagement from the America which shaped him, and in which he had placed great confidence. They help to explain, I think, why the memorial concerts held in New York in the wake of Bernstein's death seemed so charged with the bewilderment of personal loss. Most of the mourners could not have known Bernstein the man. What they sensed, however subliminally, were the damaged hopes of this most American of classical musicians.

(1993)

11 · *An Exotic Entertainment*
The Failure of American Opera

Opera in America, wrote Henry Krehbiel in 1909, would remain "experimental" until "the vernacular becomes the language of the performances and native talent provides both works and interpreters. The day is still far distant, but it will come."

New York's leading turn-of-the-century music critic, Krehbiel was a figure of awesome sagacity. His compendium *Chapters of Opera,* a chronicle of eight decades, is a tour de force of clairvoyance: its majestic assessments of new operas, and of institutions, performers, and impresarios, are bold, personal, and sure.

Krehbiel was wrong, of course, in predicting that opera in English was a cause whose day would come. But he was correct to maintain that it was a necessary cause, without which there could be no vital native repertoire to set beside Verdi, Wagner, and Bizet. Krehbiel's prognosis went further. Unless Americans grew accustomed to performing and listening to opera in the language they best understood, he predicted, American opera would remain "an exotic"—an expensive frill. Rather than spawning a central theatrical form, it would inculcate mere "craving for sensation." Boxes at the Metropolitan Opera House would remain "a coveted asset" only because they were "visible symbols of social distinction." In sum, there would be no such thing as "American opera." And there is not.

The error in Krehbiel's thinking—his assumption that Americans eventually would embrace opera in English—is understandable. After all, he had observed Frenchmen giving *Aïda* and *Lohengrin* in French, Germans giving *Faust* and *Aïda* in German, Italians giving *Faust* and *Lohengrin* in Italian—and in all cases uncontroversially, as a common practice endorsed by the composers themselves. And Krehbiel had observed a concomitant evolution of French opera, German opera, and Italian opera—of native repertory informed by native language and style. Of the singers he most admired, Jean de Reszke, schooled in Paris, was a paragon of vocal suavity and taste. Albert Niemann, coached by Wagner, placed diction and *Innigkeit* before smoothness of emission or plasticity of line. Krehbiel also admired, albeit less effusively, such formidable Americans as Lillian Nordica. But they were eclectics who represented no one school and championed no single canon.

In fact, the American disdain for opera in the vernacular is unique—Swedes, Czechs, and Hungarians have shown no comparable aversion. Stranger still, it was not always so. The further back one investigates opera in American, the more one uncovers a buried history of opera in English. During the 1890s, when New York's operatic culture was at its peak, Anton Seidl, the city's leading conductor, advocated English-language performances. So did Jeannette Thurber, who founded what was then the leading American school of music. So did Antonín Dvořák, the director of Thurber's National Conservatory of Music.

One early voice in this chorus of opinion belonged to Philip Hone, an important New York diarist, who reported on the opening of a new Italian opera house in 1833, "The performance occupied four hours—much too long, according to my notion, to listen to a language which one does not understand. . . . Will this splendid and refined amusement be supported in New York? I am doubtful." Hone also wrote, "To entertain an audience without reducing it to the necessity of thinking is doubtless a first-rate merit, and it is easier to produce music without sense than with it; but the real charm of opera is this—it is an exclusive and extravagant recreation, and, above all, it is the fashion." Of Hone's commentary, Krehbiel remarked, in *Chapters of Opera,* "The people of New York were not quite so sophisticated as they are to-day, and possibly were dowered with a larger degree of sincerity."

The charms of "music without sense" notwithstanding, opera in English made substantial early headway. English ballad opera, a species of topical spoken drama with interpolated songs, had been heard in America in the eighteenth century. Before the Civil War, English versions of Mozart, Bellini, Donizetti, Rossini, and Verdi were popular. The Pyne and Harrison English Opera Company, one of many, toured from New York to Cincinnati and Chicago, Boston to Mobile and New Orleans, performing five hundred times in one two-year period in the mid-1850s. Meanwhile, English-language grand operas were written by Americans, beginning in 1845 with William Henry Fry. By one tally, there were nearly sixty English opera troupes in the United States between 1847 and 1860.

In the postbellum decades, itinerant single-language troupes remained common. The American premiere of *Der fliegende Holländer* was given in Italian in Philadelphia in 1876. Another notable early production of the opera was toured by the English Opera Company, formed in 1873 by the noted American soprano Clara Louise Kellogg, a warmly acclaimed Senta. Kellogg documents the kind of attention to theatrical values that opera in English engendered. "One thing I had particular difficulty in learning how to handle," she recalls in her memoirs, was "Wagner's trick of long pauses." Where Senta first glimpses the legendary Dutchman, Wagner's score instructs, "She utters a loud cry of astonishment, and remains standing as if spellbound." The spell lasts many minutes, during which Senta utters not a sound. Singers of Kellogg's generation had never encountered anything comparable. Her account continues:

> "I have *got* to hold it! I have *got* to hold it!" I kept saying to myself, tightening every muscle as if I were actually

pulling on a wire stretched between myself and the audience. I almost auto-hypnotized myself; which probably helped me to understand the Norwegian girl's own condition of auto-hypnotism! An inspiration led me to grasp the back of an old Dutch chair on the stage. That chair helped me greatly, and, as affairs turned out, I held the audience quite as firmly as I held the chair.

Four years before Kellogg retired in 1887, the Metropolitan Opera House undertook its premiere season, giving opera in Italian with stellar international casts. It proved more economical, however, to become a German-language house. So in 1884–85 the Met engaged a German ensemble under Leopold Damrosch and gave everything, even *Rigoletto,* in German. When Damrosch died, in 1885, Anton Schott, one of his tenors, proposed structuring the Met as an English-language house specializing in German opera. "The plans of the present season were not entirely successful," Schott told The *New York Times.* "We are to look forward to the time when German opera will be as sacred here as in its own home"— an aspiration dictating Wagner in English. German singers, Schott promised, would be "quick to learn your own language." But his plan was not adopted, and for six more seasons the Met gave opera exclusively in German. The logic of this decision is appreciable only when one considers that New York then may well have had more German-speakers than any city after Vienna and Berlin. At the Met, opera in German *was* opera in the vernacular.

It is a little-known fact that after the company was reorganized in 1891, it eventually maintained separate orchestras and conductors for German and non-German works—no doubt engendering separate constituencies.* To a degree, these vicissitudes document continued allegiance to the custom that operas be sung in a

---

*I here generalize about a complex situation. The Met continued occasionally to do Wagner in Italian. When Anton Seidl conducted, he used his own "German" orchestra. When Luigi Mancinelli conducted, he used the regular Met orchestra.

tongue that audiences spoke. At the same time, the more glamorous and expensive opera became, the more marginalized became opera in English.

In retrospect, the American Opera Company, begun in 1885 by Jeannette Thurber, signified a mighty last-ditch effort. Never before had an American company mounted English-language productions on so lavish a scale. Thurber eschewed the "star system"; instead, she spent her money on her orchestra, chorus and ballet, sets, costumes, and stage effects. Like the Germans at the Met, she stressed an integrated musical-dramatic whole. She aspired to cut the cultural umbilical cord to Europe. Her company would perform only in English, and at reasonable prices. It would rely mainly on American singers. She hired the famous Theodore Thomas Orchestra—with the Boston Symphony, America's best. And Thomas—father of American symphonic culture, an American from the age of ten—would be her conductor.

The company's prospectus flaunted its aspirations. It would engage "the largest regularly trained chorus ever employed in grand opera in America . . . the largest ballet corps ever presented and as far as possible, American in its composition . . . four thousand new and correct costumes for which no expense has been spared . . . scenery . . . painted by the most eminent scenic artists . . . the front rank of American singers . . . supported by an ensemble which has never been equalled in this country."

Comparably ambitious was the company's season opener—not a repertory staple but Hermann Goetz's *The Taming of the Shrew*, in its American premiere, on January 4, 1886, at New York's Academy of Music. The season's fourteen other operas sampled Gluck, Mozart, Nicolai, Gounod, Meyerbeer, Delibes, Flotow, Anton Rubinstein, Wagner, Verdi, Victor Massé, and Karl Goldmark. Tour performances were given as far west as St. Louis. A second season, as the "National Opera Company," ventured all the way to San Francisco.

On balance, the American Opera was an artistic success. Orchestra, chorus, and production values were widely praised. Thomas, though not a natural theater conductor, smartly drilled his musicians. Gilded Age intellectuals believed, with Krehbiel, in an alliance of German opera with opera in English—that the first, in its Metropolitan Opera heyday, would prove conducive to the second; that Italian opera, whose prima donnas sapped financial resource and artistic nerve, would give way to musical-dramatic synthesis. A columnist for *Century Magazine* approvingly noted the "close knitting together of all the parts" at American Opera performances. *Harper's* editor George William Curtis wrote, "The opera that began with Malibran, and which has charmed generations, ended, and the German and American opera, vigorous and triumphant, sits supreme."

In genteel Boston, where bias against the star system was especially thorough, Thurber's company especially triumphed. *Lohengrin,* for example, "was performed as never before in Boston." All the artists "entered thoroughly into the spirit of the work." The chorus was fresh-voiced and well rehearsed, as well as "handsomely and picturesquely dressed and disposed in judicious masses and cleverly scattered groups." One feature "without precedent at a performance of *Lohengrin* in our local experience" was "the close and sympathetic interest manifested by the audience . . . due to the fact that the listeners understood what was sung." The crowning contribution came from Thomas's "unrivalled" orchestra, compared to which "the great Bayreuth festival orchestra can show immense perfection of drill, but not such uniformly fine executive material. . . . There was scarcely a flaw in the instrumental work from beginning to end." A second Wagner production, of *The Flying Dutchman,* amazed with its "terrifying" lightning and skillful representation of the closing wreckage and apotheosis. "Never before has grand opera been presented in this city in so complete a manner as by this troupe. We have usually had a few good singers, a poor chorus of ancient singers, a meagre orchestra of musicians who had but little enthusiasm for their work, and a poverty of scenic illustration that was often laughable. None of these faults could be laid at the door of the American Company."

These achievements notwithstanding, by mid-1887 the National Opera Company was penniless and its members, Thomas included, were suing for wages. Thurber's extravagant aspirations proved impractical—she spent too much and took in too little. Her backers, holding her fiscally irresponsible, defected. And the company had no divas or a grandiose home. It was insufficiently exotic. Henry James called opera in America "the only approach to the implication of the tiara known in American law" and "the great vessel of social salvation." The National Opera did not appeal to wealthy snobs and social climbers.

Like her conservatory director, Dvořák, Thurber understood that without government subsidies such as those European opera houses enjoyed, America could not adequately nurture an indigenous operatic culture. Though no such subsidies materialized, opera in English survived to a degree. Henry Savage, who in 1900 presented an acclaimed season of opera in English at the Metropolitan Opera House, toured a distinguished and influential English-language *Parsifal* four years later. In subsequent decades English-language opera was successfully toured by a second American Opera Company and by Boris Goldovsky, among others. New York City Opera, while never a single-language house, stresses opera in English to this day.

And yet the preponderant realty is that English-language opera did not catch on in America as foreign-born audiences died out. Seduced by questionable claims to "authenticity," and by foreign pedigrees and tongues, we have partly settled for what Philip Hone and Henry Krehbiel predicted we would not support, "an exclusive and extravagant recreation."

Perhaps the root problem is that we started too late—that an indigenous operatic culture, based on opera in English, had no time to mature. Are today's supertitles, which domesticate even Russian and Czech, an unforeseen shortcut to maturity? Or will titles doom hopes of opera in English once and for all?

Connoisseurs of Verdi's *Falstaff* should investigate a recording made in German in Leipzig in 1939, with Hans Hotter in the title role. I would not call it a "great performance," but it is memorable for reasons that are unique. Conducted by Hans Weisbach with the excellent orchestra and chorus of the Leipzig Radio, this is a *Falstaff* distinguished throughout for stylistic panache. All the singers are strong vocal personalities and vital ensemble partners. Everything argues long acquaintance with the work—but not the work as we know it. So deeply have the Germans acquired this masterpiece of Italian comic opera that it becomes a masterpiece of German comic opera, an apotheosis of Nicolai's *The Merry Wives of Windsor.*

Max Kalbeck's German *Falstaff* plays quite differently from Boito's Italian version. The sound of the orchestra is darker and more acerbic. No *Falstaff* in my experience so wickedly savors Verdi's musical irony. The vocalism is more tart than mellifluous. Arno Schellenberg, as Ford, is no plump Verdi baritone but one dryly attuned to dramatic nuance. Like an inspired Beckmesser, he finds maximum humor in emotional truth. His aria is really angry—and therefore really ridiculous.

This absence of posturing informs all the roles. Hotter's Falstaff is Jovian—even for Falstaff, larger than life. His bursts of merriment and consternation are organic, never padded. His cowardice too is real—when in Windsor Park he counts to twelve, we can easily envision his frightened face, and it is no cartoon. The signature Wotan of his generation, Hotter was also a natural comedian whose favorite parts—familiar to lucky German audiences—included Basilio in *Il Barbiere di Siviglia.*

"Wrong-language" performances, in short, not only create new roles for great vocal artists; far from being undermined by canons of "authenticity," they can shed startling perspective on the roles themselves, and on the operas they come from.

In less literal-minded times, opera in translation was taken for granted. In the opinion of W. J. Henderson, America's leading vocal authority of one hundred years ago, the greatest cast ever to undertake an American *Lohengrin,* including Italo Campanini and Christine Nilsson, sang it in Italian in New York in 1874. We don't know what Campanini's Lohengrin sounded like, but if it was anything like Fernando de Lucia's, it projected a lingering tenderness no Wagner tenor even attempts today. In his famous 1907 recording of the bridal chamber duet (as "Cessaro i canti alfin"), de Lucia envelops the music in a Mediterranean caress.

A "wrong-language" tenor who transformed all the music he touched was Julius Patzak, who can be heard on records in arias by Verdi, Massenet, and Offenbach—all sung in German, the language of the Munich Opera performances in which he took part through 1945. Patzak's 1930 version of the Kleinzach song from *Les Contes d'Hoffmann* is a tour de force of vocal acting: the crackling diction, the prickly articulation, the nasal coloration create a grotesquely suave sound picture closer to the German Hoffmann than the French Offenbach. In Patzak's 1929 recording of Alfredo's act 2 aria from *La Traviata,* the chaste timbre of his slender tenor contributes to a startling portrait of vulnerable love. The recitative, normally robust, here quietly and disbelievingly confides infatuation. (Oddly enough, this idiosyncratic performance comes closer to Verdi's metronome and dynamic markings than any we are now likely to encounter.)

Another unforgettable Verdi performance is King Philip's aria from *Don Carlo,* as recorded in 1930 by the plushest of all black basses, a voice at the same time remarkably agile and refined by impeccable diction: that of Alexander Kipnis. In Kipnis's Russian-accented German, Philip evokes the tortured and suspicious Czar Boris. The forlorn bitterness of his final exclamation imprints the words:

> Sie hat ich nicht ge*liebt*
> *Nein!* Ihr Herz bleibt *kalt*!

Purists who complain that these are not Verdi's words should be reminded that neither are

> Amor per me non ha
> No! quel cor chiuso è a me

since *Don Carlo* was composed in French, as *Don Carlos*. In fact, Verdi performances by singers like Hotter, Patzak, and Kipnis resound with tradition. These traditions may not be Italian, but they inspire, as Italian traditions could not have inspired, Germans or Russians schooled to sing in their own tongue, and therefore predisposed to make words matter in special ways.

All of this should be obvious, yet it contradicts modern practice. Before World War II singers typically learned to perform in whatever language they shared with native audiences, or at any rate in French, German, Italian, or Russian: the four dominant vocal schools, each drawing sustenance from a repertory of important French, German, Italian, and Russian operas. Only subsequently was the current, multilingual norm consolidated. (As recently as 1961, even as internationally prominent a company as Berlin's Deutsche Oper presented almost its entire repertory in German.) The shadows of performers like Hotter, Patzak, and Kipnis lie heavily on today's vocal eclecticists, whose mastery of several tongues promotes a cosmopolitan blandness as often as a mastery of several styles. A company like St. Petersburg's Kirov, performing Mussorgsky or Tchaikovsky in Russian with Russian singers, players, and conductors, materializes in New York as if from a time warp; the effortless stylistic integration of its *Queen of Spades* is an achievement as rare as it is compelling.

It was in the United States, and to a lesser degree Britain, that the principle of giving operas in the language of composition was first consistently pursued. The Met was already performing in three languages in 1895. The costs of this innovation, which helped to bury opera in English, were well understood at the time. Leading turn-of-the-century critics, performers, and educators crusaded fruitlessly to sustain an American tradition of opera in the vernacular.

Today, notwithstanding the maverick successes of Virgil Thomson, Philip Glass, and John Adams, there is no such thing as "American opera"—and, concomitantly, there are no great English-language recordings of Verdi, Offenbach, and Wagner to set beside the "wrong-language" recordings of Hotter, Patzak, and Kipnis. The very size of America's yawning opera houses, beginning with the 3,800-seat Metropolitan, reveals a failure to absorb opera as a theatrical genre rather than as a showcase for big, opulent voices. The paradigmatic American singer is a Leontyne Price or Robert Merrill, beside whom Leonie Rysanek or Tito Gobbi are flawed vocalists but magnetic singing actors. The Canadian Jon Vickers, as magnificent a singing actor as North America has produced, is the exception that proves the rule: his extensive early experience singing in English, including oratorio and opera in Canada, and opera (Bizet, Berlioz, Verdi) at Covent Garden, predisposed him to become a singer of words—like Patzak or Kipnis, a master of diction and vocal coloration.

It bears mentioning that Vickers sang in English even at the Met—not only as *Peter Grimes,* a role he indelibly marked, but as Gherman in *Queen of Spades,* Laca in *Jenůfa,* Vasek in *The Bartered Bride,* and the title role in *Samson.* As recently as the 1970s and 1980s, in fact, the Met gave English-language performances of *The Bartered Bride, Bluebeard's Castle, Dialogues of the Carmelites, Die Fledermaus, Hansel and Gretel, Jenůfa,* and *La Périchole*—not to mention the 1960s, when it presented English versions of such staples as *Boris Godunov, Così Fan Tutte, Eugene Onegin,* and *The Magic Flute.* But these departures from the original language seem unlikely to be repeated. Should they be? Singers like Gabriela Beňačková and Sergei Leiferkus, both of whom have appeared at the Met in recent seasons, sing best in Czech or Russian. On other occasions, however, American singers have been asked to "learn" Russian or Czech words phonetically. And the house up till now has opted not to use supertitles.

If opera in English nevertheless has some kind of future in the United States, New York City Opera is its most obvious venue. This company has emphasized American opera, contemporary opera, and—to a degree—opera in translation since its inception in 1944. It also has opted for supertitles, beginning in 1983. When titles translate *Die Zauberflöte* into *The Magic Flute,* they arguably confuse rather than clarify City Opera's mission. Does it make sense for a cast of young Americans to sing and speak in German for an American audience reading English words?

Christopher Keene, City Opera's general director since 1989, commands a sophisticated understanding of such questions (he himself has done translations of operas by Mozart and Henze)—and therefore volunteers no easy answers. "As a musician, I favor giving operas in the language in which they were composed," he says. "As a theater person, I consider opera in the vernacular the more trenchant and viable art. No matter how well they're coached, singers just aren't as expressive in a second or third language. When I conduct opera in English, I hear complaints after the first act that the orchestra is much too loud. That doesn't happen so much otherwise. And when opera is given in English, people pay less attention to the display of costumes, or to vocal beauty."

Speaking specifically of City Opera, Keene adds, "This company has never pursued a dogmatic policy with regard to languages. We tend to use English for operas with spoken dialogue, like *Die Fledermaus* or *The Merry Widow*—or *Die Zauberflöte,* which we give sometimes in German, sometimes in English. We tend to use English for operas in, say, Russian or Czech. But we've never done Puccini or Verdi in English. I'm always rethinking these things. Personally, I'd argue for giving *Le Nozze di Figaro* in English, as we have in the past, but there's a lot of resistance here. Also, the New York State Theater is a factor—in our house, the spoken word and sung word are so difficult to comprehend that projected titles have been a great relief to everyone."

Keene agrees that generations of American singers have suffered from inexperience singing in English, that "by and large the American artist tends to be pragmatic, facile, relatively superficial. That demonic quality you find in a Hotter or a Vickers makes Americans uncomfortable, even socially." He agrees that there is no American operatic tradition to speak of, and no great American opera. "There are some *successful* American operas, by people like Menotti, Carlisle

Floyd, and Samuel Barber. But without a system of state subsidy, we can never do what is our absolute obligation, which is to present many, many new works. You have to remember how many bad operas were composed for every *Carmen, Aïda,* or *Fidelio.*"

Should City Opera consider becoming an English-language company like London's English National Opera, which enjoys a young and vital audience and a reputation for theatrical sophistication—and whose former director of productions, David Pountney, calls projected titles "theatrical condoms"? "I go back and forth," Keene replies. "The ENO makes a statement and sticks to it—I admire that. On the other hand, I've never heard a persuasive English translation of a Puccini opera."

If there is an American road back toward opera in the vernacular, projected titles are both a shortcut and a detour. They unquestionably have facilitated a new appreciation of opera as theater. To pick the most remarkable example I know: the titles of Seattle Opera's memorable *Ring* cycle inspire a creatively detailed interpretation by a cast and production team confident that an engaged audience will understand the words. But in Seattle, as elsewhere, titles also have accompanied a curtailment of opera in English.

If opera in English is, in fact, finally doomed in the United States, the most devastating commentary on its demise may be the Met's most popular opera in English, John Corigliano and William M. Hoffman's *The Ghosts of Versailles.* Set in revolutionary France, this drama of ancien-régime class distinctions is, at first glance, no "American opera" at all. But listen to its musical pastiche, the hollow parodies of Mozart and Rossini, and *The Ghosts of Versailles* is precisely what Henry Krehbiel warned American opera would remain unless "the vernacular becomes the language of our performances": ersatz European. Or is *Ghosts* in fact a shrewd send-up, a cunning exposé of the "exotic" entertainment—"craving for sensation," lacking "high purpose" and "real artistic culture"—that Krehbiel railed against? I hope so.

(1993)

12 · *R.I.P.*

The Music of Forest Lawn

Dr. Hubert Eaton had a vision. "Cemeteries of today are wrong because they depict an end, not a beginning," he wrote in the Builder's Creed.

> They have consequently become unsightly stoneyards full of inartistic symbols and depressing customs; places that do nothing for humanity save a practical act, and that not well. I therefore prayerfully resolve on this New Year's Day, 1917, that I shall endeavor to build Forest Lawn as different, as unlike other cemeteries as sunshine is unlike darkness, as eternal life is unlike death. I shall try to build at Forest Lawn a great park, devoid of misshapen monuments and other customary signs of earthly death, but filled with towering trees, sweeping lawns, splashing fountains, singing birds, beautiful statuary, cheerful flowers, noble memorial architecture with interiors full of light and color, and redolent of the world's best history and romances.

In Glendale, California, it has been done: in place of the traditional morbidity, it is the sheer vulgarity of Forest Lawn Memorial

Park that inspires solemnity and respect. Tombstones are replaced by inconspicuous "memorial tablets" lying flush with the ground. The lawns, gardens, and terraces swarm with smiling figurines— "the largest collection of original sculpture in America." There is a museum housing a bronze tablet inscribed with the Gettysburg Address, a stone head from the Easter Islands, and a set of all the coins mentioned in the Bible. There is a gift shop that peddles large plastic walnuts with mailing labels that read: "Forest Lawn Memorial-Park In A Nut-Shell! Open me like a real nut . . ." There are replicas of famous artworks "which money cannot buy, and with which governments will not part," including "exact copies" of Michelangelo's most celebrated sculptures (the largest such collection anywhere), "the three most beautiful panels" from Ghiberti's *Paradise Doors,* and John Trumbell's *The Signing of the Declaration of Independence,* a towering 700,000-piece mosaic three times the size of the original.

All of this has been described many times over. A movie has been made about it: *The Loved One,* based on Evelyn Waugh's novel of the same name. And yet the documentation remains incomplete. Eager to relate what meets the eye (and what visitor to Forest Lawn is not?), the park's chroniclers ignore what meets the ear.

The strains I refer to are no mere icing on the casket, but an integral outcome of Dr. Eaton's policy of overthrowing "customary signs of earthly death." The idea is to make the sounds of the cemetery as pleasing and prestigious as the sights. In music, as in art, Forest lawn espouses exact reproductions of the masters—in the Church of St. Margaret of Rottingdean, where the *Andante* from Mozart's Piano Concerto No. 21 in C (K. 467), descends from a height; in the Freedom Mausoleum, where Fritz Kreisler's "Liebesleid" serenades the crypts; in the Court of David, where a symphonic condensation of the love music from Wagner's *Tristan und Isolde* issues from the flowers and bushes behind Michelangelo's *David.*

And these are preludes. The main event is far more elaborate than any incidental juxtaposition of Kreisler and Christ. To provide spiritual sustenance at Forest Lawn, Dr. Eaton's plan called for a "sacred trilogy"—dynamic renderings of "the three most dramatic moments in the life of Christ." Part one is the Last Supper Window, a stained-glass recreation of Leonardo's masterpiece. Parts two and three are gigantic oil paintings of the Crucifixion and the Resurrection. Showings of each portion of the trilogy are automated, employing a taped soundtrack in conjunction with co-ordinated lights and curtains. These multimedia presentations are the likely high points of any first tour of the grounds. They also happen to be the principle musical showcases, where passages from Wagner, Tchaikovsky, Dvořák, and other certified luminaries unfold with such bewildering pertinence as to constitute something previously unheard and unheard of: a kind of *Trauermusik* as far removed from traditional dirges, laments, and masses for the dead as surfboards are from shrouds.

"There is a dramatic story concerning the Last Supper Window," begins the taped tour guide inside the Great Mausoleum's Memorial Court of Honor, a vaulted corridor leading to a broad, curtained space.

> It began during the summer of 1924, when Dr. Eaton stood before Leonardo da Vinci's *The Last Supper,* painted on the plaster wall of an ancient Milan convent. With him was Professor Armando Vene, Royal Superintendent of Fine Arts for Italy. Through the centuries moisture had deteriorated it, and the painting, fading and flaking, was retouched time and again by lesser artists, until it was no longer Leonardo's. Both men sadly realized that soon the once-magnificent painting would be lost forever. Then, inspiration came to Dr. Eaton. Suddenly he knew there was a way to preserve Leonardo's work for posterity.

Dr. Eaton had just visited the Cathedral of Assisi, where he had seen the glowing colors wrought in glass by Rosa Casella Morelli, a young woman from Perugia. Dr. Eaton asked Rosa Morelli to recreate *The Last Supper* in stained glass for Forest Lawn. Morelli agreed: she would furnish not a copy of the decrepit wall but a reconstruction of the original painting, based on Leonardo's original sketches. Years passed. Five times the figure of Judas broke in the firing. Rosa Morelli despaired—perhaps it was not intended to be. She would try once more, and only once.

"Dr. Eaton waited, not knowing whether this Memorial Court of Honor would ever receive the window for which the huge vacant space in the wall had been planned and built. Those were anxious days, and there were sleepless nights. But at last another cable came. The Last Supper Window WAS FINISHED!"

Cued by the parting curtains, the Prelude to *Lohengrin* erupts at the very peak of its arc. The Last Supper Window stands revealed, twenty-five colored panes measuring fifteen by thirty feet. Thirteen figures, draped in reds, blues, and greens, speaking and gesticulating with frantic vigor, are outlined in black, as in a cartoon. The music subsides; the taped voice returns in an undertone: "The genius of Leonardo is nowhere so apparent as in this masterpiece. This picture does not lose its beauty as you draw closer. Instead, the details grow more distinct. Even the scales of the fish are clearly defined."

The *Lohengrin* Prelude continues to its final, *pianissimo* cymbal stroke, which yields to the *Poco Adagio* from Saint-Saëns's Third Symphony, a soothing hymn over sepulchral organ chords: "The face of Jesus is not quite complete. For THREE YEARS Leonardo tried in vain to complete his image of that face. In desperation he finally threw down his brushes, declaring, 'I do not finish the face of Christ. No man can finish it.'"

Next comes the *Largo* from Dvořák's *New World* Symphony, beginning with the familiar English horn tune: "You know the story. Who does not? This is the hour of treachery which Jesus had foretold. When they had gathered in the house, Jesus said to his disciples, 'Verily, I say unto you, one of you shall betray me.'"

To Dvořák's third subject, scored for winds over pizzicato strings, the voice intones:

> We call this the Last Supper. Yet was it not really the *first?*
> For when Jesus said, "Do this in remembrance of me," he
> gave the world a communion service which through all
> the ages has remained our Christian Thanksgiving to God,
> our grateful remembrance of Jesus Christ, and the divine
> symbol of our belief, and hope, of immortality. Thank you
> for your kind attention. Good-bye, and God bless you.

The music arrives at a long, sighing cadential passage, modulates to the major, and stops.

The Hall of the Crucifixion-Resurrection looks like a church affixed to an oversized outdoor cinema. Inside, the church is hollow and serves no evident purpose. But the adjoining auditorium really does resemble a movie theater, with cushioned seats, a sound system, and a stage bearing a curtain long enough to drape a bridge. This is where the remainder of the Sacred Trilogy is shown.

The presentation begins with a jarring extract from Richard Strauss's *Death and Transfiguration,* moving from Death's door-pounding to the first full statement of the Transfiguration theme. Then, following an interpolated timpani roll, the soundtrack produces an agitated episode (*moderato con anima*) from the second movement of Tchaikovsky's Fifth Symphony, building from *piano* to triple-*forte.* Accompanied by this great crescendo, the curtains part, and the taped guide begins: "We travel now nearly halfway around the world, backward in time nearly two thousand years. It is an overcast day outside the capital city of Jerusalem."

First Christ is revealed, a tiny central figure among hundreds of spectators atop Calvary. Next, the craggy slopes on either side of the hilltop are disclosed by the rapidly retreating fabric. Further to the right, walls, streets, a marketplace, and the principal buildings of Jerusalem race into view. To the left, half a football field away, a vast pastoral landscape unfolds, with distant houses, trees, and camels. An arrow is projected onto the canvas, and the voice returns to locate points of interest, as on a map: the winding road from Jericho, the Mount of Olives, the Palace of Herod, the tomb of David; Longinus the Centurion, the disciples Peter and John, Mary Magdalen, Lazarus, the Virgin Mary.

Incredibly, this object, "the largest religious painting in the world," stretching 45 by 195 feet, was lost for forty years. The artist, Jan Styka, could not find a buyer, nor could he afford to store a canvas that is longer than a twenty-story building is tall. Following a worldwide search, Dr. Eaton came across the forgotten picture in a New York City warehouse and brought it to Forest Lawn.

The curtains close, the music ends, the voice winds down, but there is more. In the dark, the Funeral Music from *Götterdämmerung* commences.

> Gently they placed him in the new sepulchre, wherein was never man yet laid. They mourned him, and cowered behind closed doors. . . . But the cross was not the end; it was the glorious beginning. The sacred light of Christ's Resurrection was on this day to cast its brightness upon the world, banishing the tragic darkness, and the sorrow of the crucifixion. For this was the beginning. For this is the day of the resurrection. This is EASTER MORNING.

Now Siegfried's dirge is displaced by the Prelude to *Lohengrin*—the same music that introduced the Last Supper Window, but this time from the beginning, and joined, à la Messiaen, with the twitter of chirping birds. The curtains reopen. The recorded voice lightens and quickens. A second, smaller canvas, the Resurrection, has replaced the first. Christ stands beside an open grave. In the sky, the nation of believers stretches to the horizon.

In the peace of this first Easter morning, the radiant Christ communes with God his father, who in his infinite wisdom reveals a vision to his beloved son, the results of his Crucifixion—a vision of countless millions who will follow in his wake through all centuries to come. . . . On this glorious Easter morning, the risen, radiant Christ set the world to singing, UNTO ETERNITY!!!

The tape plays the "Hallelujah Chorus." A large cross is projected onto the canvas, over the heads of the faithful. In the bottom righthand corner, enormous block letters proclaim possession of the goods: "©F L CO."

If music constitutes a particularly potent part of the Forest Lawn experience, this is because, in a graveyard piled with anomalies, it is the boldest anomaly of all. The Michelangelo copies seem apt by comparison—their subject matter is religious, and so was Michelangelo. Even the Freedom Mausoleum, with its busts of Washington and Franklin and the mosaic rendering of Trumbull's *Signing of the Declaration of Independence,* somehow fits, because God and Country are equivalently wholesome at Forest Lawn. But Tchaikovsky's Fifth Symphony and Kreisler's "Liebesleid" are as wayward here as tuxedos in a cornfield.

In this regard, the crowning incongruity is surely the music of Richard Wagner, whose ghost pervades the park as no other composer's, yet whose distaste for Christianity was so virulent he judged it incompatible with "true and living art," called hypocrisy its "salient feature," and accounted the life-on-earth it sanctions a "loathsome dungeon." At Forest Lawn, *Lohengrin* accompanies the Last Supper and the Resurrection; for Wagner, its essential source was pre-Christian myth. To underscore *David,* a twenty-foot "exact reproduction" so modest it once bore a fig leaf, Forest Lawn chooses excerpts from *Tristan und Isolde,* an opera trumpeting sins of the flesh. As for Siegfried's Funeral Music from *Götterdämmerung,* here, signifying the Savior's burial, is music for a pagan hero who murdered his stepfather and married his aunt. It is hard to know who is more offended, Wagner or Christ.

And yet no one seems offended. In fact, Wagner is absorbed as effortlessly as Michelangelo, Kreisler, and the rest. Such is the transforming power of Dr. Eaton's vision. Like Disneyland, like Los Angeles, Forest Lawn is a melting pot at room temperature, a placid brew in which any ingredient seems soluble. "Liebesleid," the Last Supper Window, and all the coins mentioned in the Bible; *Götterdämmerung, The Signing of the Declaration of Independence,* and a carving from the Easter Islands—there is something oddly uplifting about such absolute eclecticism, untroubled by irony or ennui. For initiates, this blissful coexistence of fact and fantasy, lamb and lion, Christ and Siegfried must actually be a paradise of sorts. No wonder Dr. Eaton's statues wear smiles.

A final musical allusion, conveyed in words rather than sound, accompanies *The Mystery of Life*—of all the park's sculptures, the one that strives most mightily to summarize the message of Forest Lawn. Eighteen life-size marble figures flank an actual stream of water. The figures, all naked or draped in the classical manner, include a bearded man in a turban, a boy holding a chick that has hatched in his hand, and a man with a book, scratching his head. To the side, a plaque the size of a small garage door reads:

> The Mystery of Life, largest sculptured group in Forest Lawn, has been acclaimed one of the foremost contributions of modern sculpture to the art of the world. Professor Ernesto Gazzeri carved it expressly for Forest Lawn, because Forest Lawn has solved the "Mystery of Life."
>
> In this mighty work, the figures are grouped about a mystic stream flowing from an unseen source toward an unseen destination. It raises the age old question as to the meaning of the mysterious force we call life.
>
> The exact interpretation of the whole piece, of the thoughts that rage in the minds of the various figures, is

something that has aroused many controversies. Sermons have been preached about it. There have been almost as many interpretations as there have been observers.

Meanwhile, the stream of life flows endlessly on, leaving to each his own question, to each his own answer.

At the base of the statue, a smaller plaque suggests the identities of the figures: the scientist, the learned philosopher, the atheist, the stoic, the mother and babe, the happy family group. Dr. Eaton's reading of *The Mystery of Life* is recorded on a third tablet. "During the years that the Mystery of Life group was being carved," he wrote, "the sculptor and I discussed many interpretations, but the one I like best is found in the words of Victor Herbert's immortal song:

> *Ah! Sweet mystery of life at last I've found thee,*
> *Ah! I know at last the secret of it all;*
> *All the longing, seeking, striving, waiting, yearning,*
> *The burning hopes, the joy and idle tears that fall!*
> *For 'tis love, and love alone, the world is seeking,*
> *And 'tis love, and love alone, that can repay!*
> *'Tis the answer, 'tis the end and all of living,*
> *For 'tis love alone that makes for aye!*"

To the left, from behind some shrubs, a hidden speaker plays "The Swan" from Saint-Saëns's *Carnival of the Animals.*

(1980)

· *Postlude*

Post-Classical Music in Brooklyn

As program editor for concerts at New York's 92nd Street Y through 1994, I had the good fortune to serve as artistic advisor to the "Schubertiade"—the Y's distinguished Schubert festival, anchored by the baritone Hermann Prey. One of my responsibilities was to create an annual Sunday symposium. And so I was thrust from my writer's desk—a secluded outpost, overlooking a courtyard with trees and unmolested by visitors or telephone calls—and onto the stage of the Y's Kaufmann Concert Hall.

The first Schubertiade symposium, in 1988, was a hastily organized afternoon exploring Schubert's earliest songs alongside settings by such forgotten contemporaries as Johann Rudolf Zumsteeg. The following year, "Schubert *Lieder* in Performance" was fully six hours long, starting at one P.M. and ending at eight, with a break for dinner. We considered the relevance of fortepianos, of improved ornaments, of historic recordings. The participants included the musicologist and pianist Robert Winter, the fortepianist Malcolm Bilson, the baritone Sanford Sylvan, and the critic Will Crutchfield. The day had its interesting ups and downs. The advocacy of original instruments and interpolated appoggiaturas was, I thought, more clever than persuasive. The most vivid, most spontaneous moment came in the closing panel discussion, when I pressed Prey for an opinion about the elaborate ornaments—based on ornaments once sung by Johann Michael Vogl with Schubert at the piano—we had heard sung by Timothy Mussard. "I *hated* them!" he exploded. The audience roared its approval.

The following season, in January 1990, we hit stride with "Perspectives on 'Erlkönig.'" The entire six hours were allotted to a four-minute song, Schubert's most famous composition for more than half a century after his death. How was it that "Erlkönig" made Schubert's reputation and shaped it? How assess its popularity and impact? Two lengthy presentations—each, in effect, a concert with commentary—addressed these questions. First we heard, in chronological sequence, seven settings of Goethe's poem "Erlkönig," performed by Prey and two other singers, with commentary by the musicologist Walter Frisch. The second presentation, with commentary by Frisch's Columbia University colleague Christopher Gibbs, sampled nine adaptations of Schubert's setting; here, the central performer was the pianist William Wolfram. In short, we surrounded Schubert's achievement with popular ditties and flamboyant concert works, with kitsch and *Sturm und Drang,* with music obscure and famous, all of it fostered by Goethe's ballad of 1782.

The first "Erlkönig" song turned out to be a meek strophic rendering by the actress and composer Corona Schröter, who performed it as part of the Singspiel *Die Fischerin*: a wife passes the time by singing about a child scared to death by a phantom; upon finishing, she remarks that the men are late for dinner. Equally improbable, alongside Schubert's, was the final "Erlkönig" in our survey, a Biedermeier diversion composed by Ludwig Spohr—who adds a suave obbligato violin impersonating the evil erlking. Anselm Hüttenbrenner's "Erlkönig Waltz," with its dainty hand-crossings, was a hilarious Schubert parody. In Joseph Roth's *Schubertiana,* a beer-garden medley for two violins, accordion, and guitar, snippets of "Erlkönig" and of the *Great* C major Symphony took turns with "Heidenröslein" and "Ave Maria." Of another order were Liszt's "Erlkönig"—his most famous, most virtuosic

Schubert song transcription—and the terrifying harmonics of Heinrich Wilhelm Ernst's version for solo violin. Of two other solo piano adaptations that we exhumed, Stephen Heller's "Erlkönig" proved a fascinating, free paraphrase after Schubert, and Geza Zichy's, for left hand alone, proved unplayable.

The day's most insightful comment came from an audience member who conjectured that Schubert was drawn to "Erlkönig" through bitter personal experience: Goethe's poem depicts a son who cannot share with his father what he sees and feels; there is evidence that Schubert himself was not understood by his father. The day's most electrifying moment was supplied by Prey. In his dressing room he had listened to Karen Smith Erickson sing Corona Schröter's "Erlkönig," then to Nathaniel Watson in "Erlkönig" settings by Carl Friedrich Zelter, Johann Friedrich Reichardt, and Bernhard Klein. Distinguished exponents of the Berlin *Lieder* school Goethe himself endorsed, Zelter and Reichardt support Goethe's eight stanzas gently and inconspicuously. Klein, by comparison, agitates both singer and pianist; he remolds the poem. This trajectory from reticence to skilled manipulation—a relentless "Erlkönig" drama of its own—culminated with Schubert's harrowing night ride, and with that of Karl Loewe—a famous and harrowing 1818 "Erlkönig" in its own right. With this build-up, Prey stopped the show with a rendition of the Loewe "Erlkönig" pitched at the very edge of the doomed child's abyss of terror. It was the performance of a lifetime, galvanized by a sense of occasion no ordinary format could have generated.

The Schubertiade symposiums that followed built upon "Perspectives on 'Erlkönig.'" They aimed to refresh the experience of famous music by creating a new framework for understanding. Crucial to this framework were samplings of popular music and popular culture, contradicting the solemnity of "classical music." Lectures and discussion, slides and film were incorporated. At the same time, music in live performance increasingly dominated—so that the format became that of a concert framed by topics in social and cultural history. "Schubert the Man: Myth versus Reality," in 1992, revisited portrayals of the demure, sweet-tempered *Lieder* genius: "The Music Master," an unintentionally whimsical Hollywood film biography from 1941, and *Das Dreimäderlhaus,* Heinrich Berté's phenomenally popular Schubert confection of 1916, an operetta that reinvents Schubert's life in conjunction with retooling his tunes. Prey triumphed in Tschöll's yodeling aria, performed in juxtaposition with its improbable source: the sublime E-flat *Klavierstück,* D. 946. The speakers on this occasion included Susan McClary, whose talk "Schubert's Sexuality" was a reconsideration of the *Unfinished* Symphony inspired by Maynard Solomon's contention that Schubert inhabited a homosexual subculture.

"Schubert and the Piano," in 1993, was offered in combination with Andras Schiff's traversal of the complete piano sonatas. Steven Lubin compared Schubert's E-flat Impromptu on a replica Graf fortepiano with the sound of a modern Steinway. Robert Winter dissected the first movement of the D major Sonata—and its recorded performances by Artur Schnabel and Alfred Brendel. Ruth Solie pondered the parlor piano of Schubert's day. The two-hour centerpiece was a whirlwind tour of Schubert's four-hand music by Richard and John Contiguglia, including performances of his three piano duet masterpieces from 1828. "Schubert, Death, and the Wanderer," in 1994, was a five-hour prelude to Prey's evening performance of *Winterreise.* The Germanist Cyrus Hamlin showed paintings by Caspar David Friedrich and read poems by Goethe and Hölderlin. Leon Botstein documented the heightened awareness of mortality in Schubert's disease-ridden Vienna. Susan Youens, assisted by Nathaniel Watson, argued that the *Winterreise* Wanderer does not descend into madness, but attains stoic understanding. The main event was a lecture-recital by David Owen Norris presenting the belated New York premiere of the complete Schubert-Liszt *Winterreise*—an occasion for exploring Romantic largesse in comparison to the stark proto-modern concision of Schubert's last songs.

The Schubertiade symposiums acquired a diehard following,

including followers from outside New York. They demonstrated that there exists a classical music audience starved for intellectual engagement. They demonstrated that for certain scholars academia seems as limiting as the concert regime seems to certain listeners. They demonstrated that, in combination, these scholars and listeners can create a unique opportunity for music in performance, one that showcases certain pieces and performers in special ways. Finally, they demonstrated that it was time for me to change careers.

The Schubertiade audience was unique. Its inquisitiveness set it apart. At the same time, it was undeniably aged. Its core was New York's German-Jewish audience for *Lieder* and chamber music: wonderful folks, but irreplaceable. Post-classical music needs a younger audience, one more attuned to American and contemporary culture. In New York, such an audience exists, but not in Manhattan.

The Brooklyn Academy of Music has been truly described, in *The New Yorker,* as "America's most visible showcase for experimental performance." Built in 1907, it hosted Caruso and Bernhardt, Rachmaninoff and Casals, H. G. Wells and Aldous Huxley, then declined after World War II. Its rebirth began in 1967, when Harvey Lichtenstein became executive director. As early as 1969, Lichtenstein was presenting Twyla Tharp, Robert Wilson, and Jerzy Grotowski at BAM. His commitment to vanguard performance eventually spawned the influential Next Wave Festival, beginning in 1983. Lichtenstein helped to introduce Pina Bausch, Mark Morris, and Peter Sellars—and *Einstein on the Beach, Satyagraha,* and *Nixon in China.* In 1987, he refurbished the abandoned Majestic Theater, a block away, to host Peter Brook's epic *Mahabharata.* Brook became a BAM mainstay, as did Ingmar Bergman.

Beginning in the late 1980s, Lichtenstein ventured increasingly into opera. Stressing opera as theater—his 2,000-seat Opera House is half the size of the cavernous Met—he presented stagings of Lully, Gluck, Verdi, and Weill by Jean-Marie Villegier, Harry Kupfer, Peter Stein, and Peter Sellars. He also mounted opera in the 900-seat Majestic. BAM Opera acquired a vital following. Lichtenstein was emboldened to tackle chamber and symphonic music. He made the Brooklyn Philharmonic, previously a tenant, BAM's resident orchestra in 1990. He dismantled BAM's chamber music series and invited the violinist Gidon Kremer to create something in its place. Kremer proposed a two-week chamber festival combining music, theater, cinema, opera, and dance. Lichtenstein said yes—and engaged me to help plan it.

For BAM, Kremer was a choice both obvious and inspired. His satanic intensity defamiliarizes the standard repertoire. Equally wicked are his tongue-in-cheek encores, which provoke amazed laughter and guffaws. He makes a cause of Alfred Schnittke, Sofia Gubaidulina, and Arvo Pärt—more than anyone else, he has brought to our attention these and other late twentieth-century composers from East Europe and Russia. He collaborates with Keith Jarrett and Laurie Anderson. Alongside the creamy tones and pleasing smiles of Perlman, Pavarotti, and te Kanawa, he is as discomfiting as Lenau's Mephisto fiddling with Faust. Yet his popular appeal is immediate.

For his BAM festival Kremer programmed a Moscow early music group, a chorus from Pakistan, a Soviet jazz pianist, a Cuban-American band, and a one-man Shakespeare troupe. His dual appeal—to Lincoln Center and Next Wave—promised a fusion audience that could save classical music from itself. But Lichtenstein's box office projections were poor, and he pulled out at the eleventh hour.

This disappointment proved a postponement, not a cancellation. Kremer did perform at BAM with the Brooklyn Philharmonic—after which Lichtenstein resolved that his resident orchestra, not his abandoned chamber music program, would become an experimental laboratory. I was again invited to plot strategy, and this time the plot took hold. As of 1993–94, the Brooklyn Philharmonic's main subscription season was reconceived as a series of interdisciplinary, thematically organized weekend festivals. The most ambitious were "From the New World," celebrating Dvořák's historic three-year sojourn in the United States, and "The Russian Stravinsky," exploring Stravinsky's indebtedness to folk culture. Both festivals reassessed canonized masterworks—Dvořák's *New World* Symphony, Stravinsky's *The Rite of Spring* and *Les noces*—in light of fresh research by scholars whom I knew to be galvanizing speakers. Both stretched the framework of understanding to include popular culture. Both were embellished with lobby activities and with thick, illustrated program booklets generously subsidized by the National Endowment for the Humanities.

For "From the New World," Dennis Russell Davies and the orchestra offered an aural snapshot of America's turn-of-the-century symphonic culture: the *New World* Symphony, composed in New York in 1893; the "Dirge" from the contemporaneous *Indian* Suite by Edward MacDowell, whom Americans considered their leading composer; and the *Gaelic* Symphony by Amy Beach, begun in January 1894 in response to the first Boston performance of *From the New World* less than a month earlier. The weekend proposed a thesis: that Dvořák's New World residency was more influential than we remember; and that the American music on which he drew, and which he inspired, is also worthy of remembrance. Dvořák himself was a student of African-American and American Indian music, echoes and preconceptions of which infiltrate the *New World* Symphony. In New York in 1893, all who heard this music heard its American accent, but in heated debate could not agree on its relevance to forging a native symphonic style.

At BAM we aspired to make Dvořák's American accent as audible as it seemed a century ago. In a pre-concert performance piece, Michael Beckerman recited excerpts from *The Song of Hiawatha* accompanied by excerpts from the *New World* Symphony, by way of arguing that parts of Dvořák's symphony narrate Hiawatha's wedding, his homeward journey, and his climactic battle with Pau-Pau-Keewis. Post-concert, Robert Winter presented his state-of-the-art CD ROM on Dvořák in America, including a historic recording of Harry Burleigh singing "Go Down Moses" (as he once sang it for Dvořák), and recorded reminiscences of Czech Americans who knew Dvořák during his Iowa summer of 1893. As Dvořák had told Americans that the middle movements of the *New World* Symphony were inspired by Longfellow's poem, in our performance the *Largo* and scherzo were accompanied by slides exploring resonances with the American West and Hiawatha (memorably poetic canvases by Remington and Catlin), with plantation life, and with the Bohemian homeland.

A six-hour Sunday afternoon "Interplay," modeled after the Schubertiade symposiums, revisited the debate over Dvořák's agenda for America. Juxtaposing Dvořák's *American* Suite, performed by Alan Feinberg, with a "Plantation Dance" by his African-American student Maurice Arnold, we documented the effect of the American vernacular on Dvořák's "American style." Exploring the folk pungency of certain Amy Beach songs and piano pieces, we considered the influence of Dvořák's example on a leading American composer. The afternoon's other music was by Dvořák, Burleigh, Scott Joplin, Will Marion Cook, and Arthur Farwell. The speakers included the American historian John Mack Faragher, whose words and slides recreated Buffalo Bill's Wild West (which Dvořák attended in New York) and the Kickapoo Medicine Show (which Dvořák attended in Iowa). In the lobby, during each of three intermissions, Faragher presented rare archival footage of the Buffalo Bill pageant, with its parading or warring Indians, settlers, and cavalrymen.

We kicked off "The Russian Stravinsky" with folk songs and free vodka. There were two orchestral programs plus a six-hour Sunday Interplay. Our premise was that Stravinsky—the cosmopolitan modernist who had called himself French, then resettled in California, then chose to be buried in Venice—was in fact the most Russian of Russian composers. The costumed singers and dancers of Moscow's Pokrovsky Ensemble presented folk ceremonies, including the ritual sacrifice of a virgin, underlying *The Rite of Spring;* they also sampled the regional marriage ceremonies upon which *Les noces* is based. Dennis Russell Davies and the Brooklyn Philharmonic played *The Rite of Spring.* The Pokrovskys themselves performed *Les noces*—not as a ballet, as Stravinsky intended, but as a reenacted peasant wedding. Richard Taruskin, whose landmark research paralleled years of fieldwork by Dmitri Pokrovsky, was a central participant. Taruskin and Pokrovsky agreed that Stravinsky had falsified his past and denied his borrowings in order to conceal his enduring Russianness. But Pokrovsky balked at endorsing Taruskin's view that the embittered, anti-Semitic émigré in Stravinsky impregnated *The Rite* and *Les noces* with an "anti-humanistic" political philosophy celebrating national community at the expense of individual rights.

The Brooklyn Philharmonic's 1993–94 festival weekends resulted in the highest (and most controversial) public profile in the orchestra's forty-year history. Ticket sales increased by 40 percent—from rock-bottom lows documenting an aging, alienated subscriber base. Not all the orchestra's remaining subscribers were entranced: they missed standard-format concerts with notable soloists. The new audience members, by and large, were single ticket buyers trying something different. Whatever their eventual commitment to the orchestra, they have already contributed to its redirection, as the season's last panel discussion, closing "The Russian Stravinsky," made clear.

Taruskin—a bearded, Talmudic presence—built his case patiently:

> What is Stravinsky saying about society generally? What is he telling us in the West about how we should be ordering our lives? Stravinsky had definite ideas about that, whether or not you will agree with me that they are implicit in *Les noces;* it's certainly a matter of record that Stravinsky was intensely antiliberal in his thinking at this time in his life, was traumatized by the Russian Revolution, and placed all his hopes in Mussolini as the regener-

ator of Europe. And he didn't just have Western models for this kind of proto-fascist thinking. There were good homegrown proto-fascists as well, and one of them was a very close friend of his whose name is pretty much forgotten—Lev Karsavin.

Influenced by Gogol's *Correspondence with Friends,* in which Gogol "gave voice to the most reactionary political thinking in all of nineteenth-century Russia," and by Byzantine liturgy, Karsavin theorized a "symphonic society"—"a society in which everybody's activity is ideally coordinated and harmonized with everybody else's activity, so that nobody would ever have to think, and there would never have to be a choice exercised." This was the philosophy that Stravinsky embodied in such works as *Symphonies of Wind Instruments,* which he modeled after a Byzantine service, and *Les noces,* in which the wedding celebrants behave in what is, by liberal standards, "a subhuman way."

Theodore Levin, an ethnomusicologist from Dartmouth as calming as Taruskin is needlingly self-assured, offered in response that

> one must acknowledge that *Les noces* has not in recent history been viewed as a celebration of authoritarian culture. Tikhon Khrennikov in 1948 accused Stravinsky of mocking Russian customs and animal instincts. My own feeling when I hear the work now is that Stravinsky adopts an epic voice in which he's neither celebrating nor mocking. He conveys, much as Homer did in the *Iliad,* the relentless logic of tradition, the pitiless logic of the way life is in those villages. And in that sense, I see him as a kind of ethnographer, who just reports.

The next speaker was the composer and conductor Lukas Foss, who knew Stravinsky, and who played the piano in a historic recording of *Les noces* under Stravinky's baton. "We're devoting much too much time to totally irrelevant things," Foss began in the eager *mezza voce* that excites all his conversation.

> The musicologists are so happy, in a self-indulgent way, when they can point out the influences. But that's not what's important. What's important is that the composer transforms these influences, and makes them his own. Which reminds me of a wonderful Stravinsky statement. He once said, "You must always steal, but never from yourself." What he meant by that is quite obvious. When you steal from yourself you learn nothing. When you steal from others, you enrich your vocabulary.

A flurry of applause punctuated this opinion as Foss handed the cordless microphone (a wonderful invention) to Dennis Russell Davies. Both Foss and Davies had suffered Taruskin's exegesis with visible impatience. As Davies now confided: "I said to Lukas, 'Who's going to say, "So what?"—you or me?' He said I could say it." Loud applause.

John Bowlt spoke next. He is a historian of Russian visual art, a specialist in the Diaghilev circle, of which Stravinsky was part. He sailed round the musicians' debates:

> I feel that all these comments about structure and derivations that we've heard are of course very important. But when you come down to it there's something in Stravinsky which is profoundly incomprehensible and, well, perhaps divine. There is suddenly a sensibility that moves us beyond words. And it's exactly the same kind of experience I've had when I look at the black square of Malevich of 1915, or hear "e u iu/i a o/o a/o a e e i e ia," which is a transrational poem of 1913.

Elizabeth Valkenier took the microphone and briefly observed: "Being a specialist in nineteenth-century Russian social history, all I would like to add is that this discussion—in which there is only one answer to a question, and anything else has to be pulverized—is also profoundly Russian."

Taruskin now requested the microphone and commenced:

I of course disagree fundamentally with what we've been hearing. And I think these are very important issues. I really feel a moral commitment to say something, even though I doubt that many of you will agree with me. The idea that it is somehow an attack on the composer, or a diminishment of his work, to bring up what we are accustomed to think of as extramusical factors that bear upon it, especially when these are things that we don't normally regard as wholesome—I think it's a kind of evasiveness. There's something that makes us uncomfortable about attaching political meanings to a musical work, especially if they're not political meanings we learned in school to admire. Am I in fact writing off the work? Am I in fact disengaging myself from commitment to it by raising these points? Just the contrary. The reason I became interested in such questions is that I find *Les noces* the most moving experience that twentieth-century music has to offer. And I think unequivocally that it is Igor Stravinsky's masterwork. When I listen to it I have goosebumps from beginning to end, and in a good performance I shed tears. And yet *Les noces* is abhorrent to me in some ways. The content is abhorrent and the experience is intensely compelling. It creates within me a conflict, it creates within me a tension. And that is what has impelled me to do the research that I've done.

As moderator of this discussion, I had been wrestling with the impulse to interrupt, to compress and simplify. But it had proceeded so spontaneously—with barely a pause for breath—that I only now interceded to inquire if there were questions or comments from the audience. To my astonishment, a forest of hands—easily fifty, maybe seventy-five—shot up. We ended an hour later only because we had to clear the stage—after which the discussants continued in smaller groups. This experience violated every precept conveyed by the sound bite. It contradicted the disdain for complexity inculcated by anchormen and talk show hosts, politicians and campaign advisers, media experts and classical music broadcasters. It demonstrated that an audience attending a 1994 Stravinsky festival at the Brooklyn Academy of Music could listen with relish and discernment to a debate over the relevance of Lev Karsavin to *Les noces*—a debate, moreover, whose flair and subtlety of expression would not have disgraced Fleischmann's round table and other Union Square haunts frequented by the likes of James Gibbons Huneker, Anton Seidl, and Antonín Dvořák a century ago.

The 1993–94 Brooklyn Philharmonic season generated collaborations with Da Camera of Houston and with the Chicago Symphony. The 1994–95 Brooklyn Philharmonic season, meanwhile, includes Dennis Russell Davies conducting Philip Glass, Marianne Faithfull singing Kurt Weill—and Gidon Kremer performing Pärt and Schnittke.

My 1987 book, *Understanding Toscanini,* was a declaration of symphonic obsolescence. Subtitled "How He Became an American Culture-God and Helped Create a New Audience for Old Music," it argued that the American concert orchestra—a remarkable invention, distinct from the pit orchestras of Europe—lost its way during the interwar decades. An expanded audience, full of upwardly mobile newcomers; a new compositional aesthetic, hostile to Romantic pleasures; an influx of luminary performers, chased west by Hitler, yet retaining European artistic loyalties—these were some of the factors dictating that canonized masterpieces and celebrity conductors dominated as never before. America's orchestras turned hostile to American music, to contemporary art, to creativity itself.

The glamour of what Marc Blitzstein derisively called the "Platinum Orchestra age" was guaranteed not to last. The celebrity conductors died off. The canonized repertoire grew old and overly familiar. Blitzstein was not the only American composer who saw it coming; they all did. Daniel Gregory Mason decried "museums of the past" and "fashion-enslaved, prestige-hypnotized minds." Virgil Thomson lampooned popularizers for whom Great Music ended with Sibelius. Aaron Copland despaired of the American obsession with "masterworks."

By the 1980s the complacency of the classical music establishment was stultifying—except to the administrators and music businessmen who preserved the status quo. The only thing that worried them was their aging audience. A 1982 survey by the New York Philharmonic found that 51 percent of its listeners were over fifty-five years old, with only 13 percent under thirty-five, and 69 percent reporting annual incomes of forty thousand dollars and more. Two years later, the Philharmonic undertook a characteristic response: a marketing study. The study's recommended "strategies," equally characteristic, were for improved marketing. As I reported in *Understanding Toscanini:*

> Acknowledging audience antipathy to "new music" as documented in the 1982 survey, the study at no point conjectured that fresher repertoire might entice younger listeners; rather, the orchestra's "image" needed freshening. Alluding to widespread disenchantment with the music director in the musical press, the study inferred that "bad publicity" needed rectifying by "increased publicity support, particularly in the form of selected appearances and interviews by Mr. Mehta and—wherever possible—members of the orchestra." The "Philharmonic experience," according to the study, aspired to fulfill leisure needs by furnishing an "enjoyable" and "stress-reducing activity." How to communicate the Philharmonic experience? "[Get] on the air more frequently in the New York area

. . . in TV and cable and radio." "High visibility [for] New York occasions, like the Big Ship parade, a dedication of the Statue of Liberty, a Christmas Show, a New Year's Eve concert, etc." "Solo appearances by members of the Philharmonic with other area orchestras." "Further development of the management of direct mail and telephone marketing by zip code areas."

Thus did the manipulable needs and aspirations of the classical music audience preempt the needs and aspirations of art. But this survival strategy could only prove self-defeating in the long run.

In 1992, the American Symphony Orchestra League published a three-part study of the condition of American orchestras. A year later, a follow-up report, "Americanizing the American Orchestra," called for substantial and systemic change embracing repertoire, format, and the relationship to the community.

At recent ASOL conventions, self-congratulation, once a frequent theme, has been displaced by ferment—by a plethora of reports on new tactics for audience development, for music education, for transforming the concert experience. Some proposed strategies seem desperate or expedient: old goods repackaged. But, even where imagination falters, the search is authentic, not cynical.

A new subject matter—a diversified "post-classical music"—is an inescapable outcome of these tendencies if they are to do the work of renewal. What the searchers are groping toward is an integration of concert music and society unknown since the turn of the century, when Dvořák studied African-American spirituals, American Indian chants, and Stephen Foster songs, and Anton Seidl led the *New World* Symphony for a public eager to participate in the quest for an American music.

In *Understanding Toscanini,* I mapped five "worlds of American music" that had been omitted from the curriculum of music appreciation—and therefore withheld from the new interwar audience and its progeny.

> The first was of Koussevitzky, Tanglewood, and [the interwar journal] *Modern Music:* the American composers of the twenties and thirties. The second was a maverick sidebar to the first: rangy American originals in the tradition of Whitman and Melville, beginning with Charles Ives and including Edgard Varèse, Harry Partch, and John Cage. The third omitted world was of American musical theater: Gershwin, Cole Porter, Irving Berlin, Richard Rodgers. The fourth—endorsed by *Modern Music,* Ives, and Gershwin, denigrated by highbrow music appreciators—was jazz, its precursors and forms: gospel, blues, ragtime, swing. The fifth omitted world of music mounted the most thorough attack on the "masterwork" idea, with its elaborate distinctions between "serious" and "popular," "art" and "recreation." Propagated in *Modern Music* by the composers Henry Cowell, Paul Bowles, and Colin McPhee, among others, it prophetically embraced the music of Asia, Africa, and South America, accommodating listening modes more meditative or ceremonial than those of the modern West. . . . McPhee's *Tabuh-Tabuhan* (1936)—his best-known composition, forecasting the "minimalism" of Steve Reich and Philip Glass—is an orchestral toccata appropriating Balinese gamelan techniques.

Seven years later, our Brooklyn Philharmonic programs at BAM embrace Virgil Thomson, Charles Ives, Kurt Weill (in both his Berlin and Broadway modes), Duke Ellington, Colin McPhee, and Philip Glass. They debunk the distinction between high and popular culture. Rather than elevating Great Music and Great Performances, they leaven Mozart and Stravinsky with large helpings of folk music and jazz. And this assault on "classical music" is not a premeditated strategy, but a natural direction dictated by the orchestra's venue, its audience, its time and place.

And we are not alone. Across the river, in Manhattan, Leon Botstein has reinvented the American Symphony Orchestra. American Symphony concerts investigate such topics as "Bruckner and the 20th Century" and, in conjunction with the Metropolitan Museum of Art, "Paris in the 1860s: The Origins of Impressionism." Every August, the orchestra anchors the Bard Festival, whose intellectual ambitions are no less enthralling than its bucolic setting.

Quest and discovery equally prevail at the Baltimore Symphony's Saturday morning Casual Concerts, where David Zinman conducts not Beethoven's Fifth and *Rhapsody in Blue,* but Mahler's Sixth, Elgar's First, and Michael Torke's *Ash.* No less than his uncompromising repertoire, Zinman's maniacal humor subverts. When he sings "Full Moon and Empty Arms" in his high plaintive baritone, he not only illustrates that Rachmaninoff's melodies "could be popular songs," but creates an opportunity for madness: a Casual Concerts contest. "We want you to send us your lyrics to any Rachmaninoff tune," he announces; he intends to pick and perform the winning entry. Discussing Brahms's First Symphony, he features "News from the Trombone Section." "Did you know that in Brahms's First Symphony, the trombones don't play at all until the fourth movement? What do you suppose they're doing all that time? Come with me. We're going to head back to the trombone section and talk to them." Threading his way through cellos and winds, he winds up face to face with four trombonists. "Gentlemen, you're in the special teams division. You sit there for a long time and do nothing. Obviously you can't read a book, because people are looking at you. You can't scratch yourself. What do you think about?"

Zinman relishes comedy for its own sake. But by smashing pedestals he also honors the Great Composers thus toppled to earth: listening to Rachmaninoff, listening to Brahms, listening to Mahler, his Saturday morning audience is provoked to hear in ways that are anything but casual. Baltimore's "casual" concertgoers pore through the program notes. They rise to the challenge of new music. They compose lyrics for Rachmaninoff's tunes.

Granted, these are initiatives that seek to make a virtue of necessity. Like the Brooklyn Philharmonic, the American Symphony is fighting for survival in a city oversupplied with concerts, musicians, and orchestras. Similarly, the Baltimore Symphony, which promises its musicians more than three hundred services per season, created a Saturday morning series in an attempt to add concerts without depleting its existing market. And yet when Zinman says that "the days of simply sitting at concerts are vanishing," what he perceives is less a problem than an opportunity. His reforms, like Botstein's, are activated less by a marketing plan than by an artistic vision—and the faith that marketing will follow, because the essential crisis is one of substance, not appearances.

The Baltimore Symphony's Casual Concerts have succeeded in drawing a younger audience. Will the Brooklyn Philharmonic also succeed? The Manhattan audience that flocks to BAM for contemporary dance, theater, and opera dismisses orchestral concerts as old-fashioned and redundant; this plausible stereotype is tough to puncture. In Brooklyn, meanwhile, former Philharmonic subscribers long for bygone comforts. How should they be wooed? What is the orchestra's largest potential audience? What is its most appropriate audience?

As of this writing, these questions still need answers. But other answers are emerging. In 1987, in *Understanding Toscanini,* I searched for evidence that a new audience for symphonic music could materialize outside traditional precincts, and beyond conventional expectations. Seven years later, I find that I can glimpse the possibility of a post-classical future.

▪ *Notes on Sources*

In my "Introduction: The Post-Classical Predicament," James Gibbons Huneker quotes are from Huneker, *The New Cosmopolis* (New York, 1915), pp. 69, 75–78, 81; Huneker, *Steeplejack* (New York, 1920), vol. 2, p. 68; Henry Finck, ed., *Anton Seidl: A Memorial by His Friends* (New York, 1899; reprint, New York, 1983), pp. 115–16. Reporter likened Huneker to *Encyclopedia Britannica* in *New York Times,* February 20, 1921 (section 3, p. 14). On Anton Seidl, see Joseph Horowitz, *Wagner Nights: An American History* (Berkeley and Los Angeles, 1994), especially pp. 125–37, 211. Arthur Farwell, "America's Gain from a Bayreuth Romance: The Mystery of Anton Seidl," *Musical Quarterly,* October 1944. Krehbiel, Henderson, and Russell quotes from Joseph Horowitz, *Understanding Toscanini* (New York, 1987; reprint, Minneapolis, 1988; reprint, Berkeley and Los Angeles, 1994), pp. 60, 61, 100, 263. Burrian quote from Horowitz, *Wagner Nights,* pp. 273–74.

"Mozart as Midcult: Mass Snob Appeal" was first published in *Musical Quarterly,* Spring 1992. Copyright 1992 by Oxford University Press; used with permission. On Russell's films, see John Hanke, *Ken Russell's Films* (Metuchen, N.J., 1984). The most recent reprinting of Dwight Macdonald's "Masscult and Midcult" is in Macdonald, *Against the American Grain* (New York, 1983); the original version was in *Partisan Review,* Spring 1960. Peter

Shaffer quotes from Shaffer, "Paying Homage to Mozart," *New York Times Magazine,* September 2, 1984. Tchaikovsky letter quoted in David Brown, *The Crisis Years,* vol. 2 of *Tchaikovsky: A Biographical and Critical Study* (New York, 1982), pp. 146–51. Susan Sontag, "Notes on Camp," reprinted in *A Susan Sontag Reader* (New York, 1983).

"Of Swimming and Dancing: On Staging Wagner's *Ring*" was first published in *Opus,* April 1987. *Nietzsche Contra Wagner,* trans. Walter Kaufmann, in *The Portable Nietzsche* (New York, 1954). Thomas Mann, *Pro and Contra Wagner,* trans. Allan Blunden (Chicago, 1985).

"Dvořák and the New World: A Concentrated Moment" was first published in Michael Beckerman, ed., *Dvořák and His World* (Princeton, 1993), and is reprinted with permission. For background on Jeannette Thurber, see Emmanuel Rubin, "Jeannette Meyers Thurber and the National Conservatory of Music," *American Music,* Fall 1990. For background on Anton Seidl, see Joseph Horowitz, *Wagner Nights: An American History* (Berkeley and Los Angeles, 1994). Dvořák's essay on Schubert appeared in *Century Magazine,* July 1894. For relevant Dvořák writings, see Michael Beckerman, ed., *Dvořák and His World.* Beckerman's expertise in Dvořák was invaluable in preparing this article.

"The Transcendental Ives" is adapted from the Brooklyn Philharmonic Orchestra program booklet for "American Transcendentalists," November 1994. My commentary is particularly indebted to Frank Rossiter's *Charles Ives and His America* (New York, 1975). Stuart Feder's psychoanalytic biography, *Charles Ives: "My Father's Song"* (New Haven, 1993), is another version of my perspective of a composer reinhabiting the past. Most of the quotations may be found in Vivian Perlis, ed., *Charles Ives Remembered* (New Haven, 1974).

"Mahler, Klimt, and Fin de Siècle Vienna" was first published in *Keynote,* September 1986. For relevant background on Klimt (and many pertinent illustrations), see Carl Schorske, *Fin-de-Siècle Vienna: Politics and Culture* (New York, 1980).

"The Composer as Emigrant: Korngold and Weill, Hollywood and Broadway" is adapted from program notes for the Los Angeles Philharmonic, March 1991. Reprinted with the permission of the Los Angeles Philharmonic Association. My commentary on Weill, including quotes from Brecht and Canetti, draws upon Stephen Hinton, ed., *The Threepenny Opera,* a Cambridge Opera Handbook (Cambridge, Eng., 1990), and Stefan Zweig, *The World of Yesterday* (New York, 1943).

"The World's Greatest Piano Career: The Transformations of Vladimir Horowitz" was first published as "Letter from New York: The Transformations of Vladimir Horowitz" in *Musical Quarterly,* Fall 1990. Copyright 1990 by Oxford University Press; used with permission. Thomas Frost quoted in the *New York Times,* April 22, 1990. Howard Taubman's articles appeared in the *New York Times Magazine,* October 17, 1948, and January 11, 1953. Samuel Chotzinoff on Horowitz in *A Little Nightmusic* (New York, 1964), pp. 44–45. Asafyev quotation from *Critical Essays and Reviews* (Moscow: Muzika, 1967), Horowitz and Byron Janis quotations in Glenn Plaskin, *Horowitz* (New York, 1983), especially pp. 236–38, 246.

"Precision Engineering: Glenn Gould and the Phonograph" was first published as "The Improbable Wagnerian" in the *New York Times,* June 16, 1991. Copyright 1991 by The New York Times Company. Reprinted by permission. The CD under review was Sony SK 46279.

"The Worldliness of Nathan Milstein" was first published as "The Complete Cosmopolite" in the *New York Times,* August 22, 1993. Copyright 1993 by The New York Times Company. Reprinted by permission. The recordings under review were "The Art of Nathan Milstein," EMI ZDMF 64830, and Bach sonatas and partitas, EMI ZDMB 64793.

"The Teachings of Leonard Bernstein" was first published as "Professor Lenny" in the *New York Review of Books,* June 10, 1993. Reprinted with permission from *The New York Review of Books.* Copyright 1993 Nyrev, Inc. For a history of the music appreciation movement, see Joseph Horowitz, *Understanding Toscanini* (New York, 1987; reprint, Minneapolis, 1988; reprint, Berkeley and Los Angeles, 1994), pp. 189–213; I am also indebted to Paul DiMaggio, of Princeton University, for sharing with me his perusal of music-educational materials. Bernstein's Harvard bachelor's thesis was published as "The Absorption of Race Elements into American Music" in Leonard Bernstein, *Findings* (New York, 1982). Scripts for twelve of Bernstein's *Omnibus, Ford Presents,* and *Lincoln Presents* television programs may be found in his books *The Infinite Variety of Music* (New York, 1966) and—a superior collection—*The Joy of Music* (New York, 1959). The programs themselves, as well as all of Bernstein's Young People's Concerts, may be viewed at New York's Museum of Television and Radio.

"An Exotic Entertainment: The Failure of American Opera" was first published in *Opera News,* November 1993. For more on the American Opera Company, see Joseph Horowitz, *Wagner Nights: An American History* (Berkeley and Los Angeles, 1994).

"R.I.P.: The Music of Forest Lawn" was first published as "The Music of Forest Lawn Memorial-Park" in *Keynote,* January 1980.

· Index